CLUBS*DRUGS AND CANAPÉS

CLUBS*DRUGS AND CANAPÉS

A deep journey into the shallows of the night

Nick Valentine

unbound

This edition first published in 2013

Unbound
4–7 Manchester Street, Marylebone, London, W1U 2AE
www.unbound.co.uk

Typeset by Lorna Morris
Cover design by Kevin Carvill
Cover photography by Nick Rhodes

A CIP record for this book is available from the British Library

ISBN 978-1-78352-012-1 (PB)
ISBN 978-1-78352-011-4 (EB)

Printed in England by Clays Ltd, Bungay, Suffolk

For DODO, TOM, JANE and SKID

'…the best of life is but intoxication.'
LORD GEORGE GORDON BYRON

'And the worst is even better.'
NICK VALENTINE

PROLOGUE

'Do you fancy a five-day jolly to help organise a boat party in Cannes during the film festival?'

'Do champagne corks pop?'

~

An early morning flight from London to Nice, a shit-shaking helicopter transfer and here I am at the Grand Hotel du Cap Ferrat. This luxurious destination venue for the 'international elite' was established in 1908 and makes Rodeo Drive look like the Old Kent Road.

Among the palms and princesses, I enjoy a rather boozy working lunch with my host/employer. We discuss the celebrity guest list, entertainment and running order for the forthcoming event. Job done! Kylie Minogue, dining on the next table, joins us for dessert, an overly rich chocolate mousse.

An afternoon speed-tanning by the pool, a short disco nap, a stinging shower and it's time to check out the nightlife across the border.

Monaco is an uber-glamorous, sunshine-soaked, independent and jet-set city-state nestled in the bosom of the French Riviera. It's super-yacht heavy, tax-free and the gilded stomping ground of a playboy prince. Albert II, Prince of Monaco, is the only son of Prince Rainier and the American Academy Award-winning actress Grace Kelly, and heir to the principality. The Royal House of Grimaldi has ruled this billionaires' playground since 1207. It's the second smallest country in the world after the Vatican, yet one of the richest.

My first port of call is the legendary Sass Café, a restaurant/ piano bar off the Boulevard du Larvotto. A few mango Martinis, a quick bite to eat and I'm ready for take-off.

Next stop – Jimmy'z, a famed, coastal nightclub, where the

super-rich and their wealthier friends come to party. There's a restaurant, there's a bar, there's an ornamental pond. Film stars rub shoulders with Formula 1 drivers. Size zero 'resting' models laugh exaggeratedly at punchlines they can neither hear nor understand. Short men escort Amazonian trophies, every step a red carpet strut.

'He's a lot taller when he stands on his oil bonds,' a Riviera regular tells me over beer nuts, pointing in the general direction of a young, diminutive Tom Cruise lookalike.

My NBC – New Bar Companion – is smoking Marlboro Reds like a neurotic cowboy on death row. He says he works in construction, hotels mainly.

'Dubai's where you want to stick your money right now!'

'Oh, really?'

I politely take my leave, give the size 12s a quick workout under the pulsating strobes and rejoin my crew.

My host/employer's drinking table is full of long-legged, Jimmy Choo clad, plastically enhanced Euro beauties who all make the cast of *Baywatch* look like the cast of *Crimewatch*. I'm chilling. I'm smiling, giving it the full Detroit lean on the vacant seat to my left. We're all drinking vintage bubbles at 'no way!' a bottle and compounding the kidney damage with flavoured vodka chasers. The dance floor is filling up with Venus' finest, one eye on the time, the other eye on the money. Life's not bad. Not bad at all. The waiter passes me the menu.

'No, I'm fine, thanks.'

'No sir, is the bill, we're closing.'

I scan the room for my host. He's nowhere to be seen. I pop to the loo. Empty! Back to the table, head held low. The waiter is hovering like Peter Rachman on rent day. I nervously open the soft buckskin folder. Either I'm seeing triple, or there's five zeros worth of party juice to settle. I'm going to be washing dishes until the world stops spinning and then some.

The three previous hours of carousing suddenly feel a lot less sexy, as all the heavily made-up faces at the table turn towards to me. Out of the corner of my eye I see a heavyset man mountain approach the waiter. They're chatting, they're laughing. I'm silent, I'm sweating… profusely. The waiter leans in for the kill.

'Is ok sir. Bill is taken care of.'

Man mountain winks at me. Thank fuck, I recognise him now. He works for my dear departed tycoon.

'I'll get the next one then.'

REWIND
If the events aren't exactly chronological, well...

I suppose it all started when my mother met Steve and Peta, a temporary homeless couple, at the Railway Tavern one boozy Sunday lunchtime. A good few snifters later, my old dear suggested they come and live with us in suburban Teddington. This was not unusual for my mother. Her idea of a takeaway was bringing home the last person to get a round in. Our spare room was like a Travelodge for lost souls. Teddington, or Tedders as it was affectionately known by its inhabitants, is famous for being the birthplace of Noël Coward and the location of the National Physical Laboratory, where my mother worked as a secretary.

'It's great, Nick. Steve's an experienced bass player and said he'll teach you.'

I have just bought my first bass guitar (paid for with a six-month paper round) and formed The Poseurs, a weekend punk band.

Oh shit, I'm thinking, some sad muso from the local pub band is gonna bore my arse off.

'Oh, yes, he used to play in a band in the early 70s.'

It's now 1978. Here we go.

'T. Rex.'

Well, fuck me sideways, they're my favourite band.

'That's my favourite band.'

'I thought The Partridge Family were.'

'No, erm... They *used* to be.'

My puppy pop past has come back to haunt me and my punk credentials are in tatters before I've even played my first bum note.

Twenty minutes later, an old Land Rover pulls in to our drive. Out jumps an extremely jovial Steve Currie and an attractive blond in her mid-to-late twenties.

'Hi, I'm Steve, this is Peta. You must be Nick. Grab this, will you!'

He passes me the white Fender Precision bass that Marc Bolan bought for him after a huge bust-up on their last Japanese tour.

And so it comes to pass. I'm royally star-struck. Steve's had loads of Top 10 hits, played Wembley Empire Pool, hung out with Elton John, David Bowie and Rod Stewart, and had his body massaged by three Japanese groupies, using their pussies as loofahs, on that last Japanese tour.

'When's my first lesson, Steve?'

A few days later, Steve mistakenly mixes up our dining-room table with his bed and enlists Peta's help to polish the mahogany top. This is going to be fun. Our new housemates sure know how to party, and party they do, aided and abetted by my mother and father. One day, however, the revelry comes to a dramatic and abrupt end when my mother dies unexpectedly of a blood clot on the brain. She is 51. The snaking cavalcade of grief on the rainy, mournful day of her funeral mistakenly pulls up to the cemetery instead of the crematorium. My older brother Rod (by seven years), who has now changed his name to the more rock 'n' roll sounding Skid Marx and formed Blast Furnace and the Heatwaves with the *New Musical Express* staff writer Charles Shaar Murray, addresses our tearful relatives.

'Don't worry, everybody… they'll put her on simmer.'

Steve and Peta head off solemnly for Portugal. Steve leaves behind one of his gold discs for my safe keeping and plenty of priceless memories.

A few years later, he misjudges a treacherous corner on a coastal road in the Algarve and, in a macabre echo of Marc Bolan's death, suffers a fatal car crash. His spirit, however, stays with me to this day.

~

I'm 16. I'm on stage with my new band The Pedestrians (The Poseurs split up when our second rehearsal clashed with the drummer's chess club picnic). Cherry red, imitation Gibson SG bass, skinny black jeans, mutated dogtooth jacket and winkle-pickers that pinch like a matador's arse-ring on fight day. No matter. I've discovered my reason for being. This is where I belong. This is why I exist.

~

I spent so much time with Steve listening to his stories and so little time learning bass that I'm still utterly crap, but it doesn't matter. I've seen The Clash play at the Music Machine, a run-down, live music dive in Camden and the experience has changed my life. Paul Simonon, their bass player, is pretty shit, too, but he's also the coolest motherfucker south of the North Pole.

~

At The Clash gig, Glen Matlock, the ex-Sex Pistols bass player, got a right old battering from the bouncers two feet in front of me for no apparent reason and I crashed my brand new, electric blue Suzuki AP 50 moped on the way home and ended up on the snow-covered roof of a brand new MG. Quite an eventful night, really. I bought the bike on hire purchase, so will probably still be paying it off when The Clash start drawing their pension.

~

Meanwhile, back on stage, I'm so short-sighted (and glasses and punk rock do not go together) that I can't see past the first row. In fact, I don't even know if there is a second row, but the spit from the audience is reaching its intended target... me. In spite of this, I find the whole experience incredibly exhilarating.

~

My old man, who is the local copper, dropped me off at the gig tonight in his police panda car, so I had to get him to pull up 100 yards from the venue and pretend to 'leg it from the old bill'. Punk and police fathers don't go together either.

~

It's been a week since I left school (a nondescript comprehensive in Hampton). I've answered an ad for a trainee film technician in

The Richmond and Twickenham Times. My father thinks doing A-levels would be an unnecessary indulgence. He left school when he was 13.

~

I smashed the interview and got offered the job on the spot; £26 a week and luncheon vouchers. I've arrived.

~

My father Tom has rather generously let me have a gap weekend before starting work on Monday.

~

Six months as a trainee 'white, two sugars please' film technician has not quite lived up to my expectations, so a quick trip to the Job Centre and I'm now a trainee surveyor. I spend the whole day holding a wooden rod as vertical and still as I can manage, while the surveyor takes a tacky point reading. As the company that I'm now gainfully employed by has a Home Office contract, my tacky points are all in HM prisons. Technically I'm too young to be here, but the security is surprisingly slack.

~

Today's lunch in HM *Shitsville* is being served by Captain Birdseye (he chopped up his family and put them in the freezer) and Dirty Dolittle (I don't want to know the reason for that nickname) is on tea duties. Not really for me… Next!

~

I'm at Teddington Library going through an A to Z of potential careers. I've got as far as N for Nurse without anything jumping out at me.

~

A Scritti Politti gig at the Africa Centre with my friend Anna Goodman who works in Kensington Market, the style mecca for London's fanzine generation, where clothes run the whole Henry Ford colour spectrum. Tonight, Anna's gone for the Cruella Deville look while I'm in my customised Millets boiler suit; a total nightmare every time you need to take a leak.

~

Back at the library. Up to R for Roofer. A couple of pages away from Y for You Really Should Have Revised For Your Exams.

~

Another concert, this time at the Electric Ballroom. I'm on my own, but it's a great line-up with The Specials, Madness and The Selector all on the bill. The downside is, is the place seems to be full of skinheads and the atmosphere is really heavy. I love The Specials, but I'm going to bail while I still can.

~

I'm on the Tube at Camden Town station waiting for it to leave. A large group of skins are trying to kick open the closed doors. It's a frenzied blur of Harringtons and Doctor Martin soles.

'Kill the punk, kill the punk.'

The driver keeps tantalisingly pulling away, then stopping. I'm shitting myself. Please go, please go, please go…

~

We're on our way. I can hear my heart crashing against my rib cage. I didn't used to have this trouble at Bay City Roller gigs.

~

Skid's bought me skintight leather trousers for my 17th birthday. I've got chicken legs. David Cuff, The Pedestrians' guitarist who

I've known since I was four, wants to know, 'What's with the flares?' The band's over. Sartorial differences.

~

Skid's musical career as a blues harmonica player has also stalled. His band's brand of pub rock/rhythm and blues has been aggressively swept aside by punk rock and they've sadly gone straight from 'will-bes' to 'has-beens' without really getting their just deserts. A bad case of wrong time, right place, really.

~

Joy upon joy. I started a new job today as a trainee paste-up artist at DDM, an advertising agency in Ladbroke Grove. Skid's been freelancing here since graduating from Harrow on the Hill Art College and has somehow managed to wangle me a kind of apprenticeship; £44 a week and they have agreed to pay for me to study graphic design one day a week at the London College of Printing in Farringdon (and not a shitty tacky point in sight).

~

Paste-up suits my and Skid's personality to a tee. Making scraps of paper sit square on a page (PCs and Macs are yet to be invented), drawing the odd key line and cleaning it all up with a squirt of lighter fuel. It's as finicky as fuck, but the perfect job for the anal retentive.

~

My brother reckons we should form a tribute band and call it OC/DC.

~

After obsessive compulsive disorder, another trait Skid and I both share is constant list-making. I make lists about making lists. My father's the same. My sister Jane says I put the 'lyst' in 'you need to see an analyst'.

~

My granddad once had a nervous breakdown and ended up in Shenley Psychiatric Hospital, which was once discourteously known as a 'colony for mental defectives'. On my first trip to see him, he kept telling me to 'hang in there'. The doctor told me later that my grandfather thinks I'm the patient and he's the visitor.

~

I got picked up on the Tube on the way to work today by a German Debbie Harry lookalike. She likes my new bleached barnet and red brothel creepers. I can't quite believe it. Lena's 12 years older than me, ridiculously hot and wants to know if I've started shaving yet (I haven't).

~

A drink with Lena at her local music venue. The Police are headlining. She introduced me to Sting on his way to the stage, but he was rubbernecking at the time and failed to acknowledge me. By compensation, Lena's invited me back to her flat in Olympia after the show, which is now going painfully slowly.

~

We have finally made it back to Lena's. Sex is quicker than the time it takes me to open the condom packet. I haven't mentioned to Lena that I'm still a virgin. She's still in the process of undressing by the time I hit the Imperial Leather and the power shower.

~

I once came dangerously close to losing my virginity during my penultimate year of school. Upon hearing that David Cuff and I had yet to pop our cherries, one of the more physically advanced girls in our art history class rather generously offered her services for the job. An arrangement was duly made to meet at her house later that evening, her parents being otherwise occupied with the weekly Sainsbury's shop. When we excitedly arrived at her pebbledashed semi at the designated time, our hearts aflutter, we were greeted with the somewhat confusing and incredibly disappointing sight of an orderly queue of eager, pubescent classmates, stretching from the front gate right up to our benefactor's single bedroom. It seemed the object of our unmitigated desire had been somewhat over-generous with her invites.

'Oh well, if we cycle fast enough, we can still catch the first episode of the new series of *Happy Days*.'

~

I spent my day at the London College of Printing choosing typefaces to represent wild animals and deciding what colour represented my personality. I felt like I was back in Sunday school. Not quite what I imagined art college to be like. My advertising agency interior resembles the Stock Exchange. The college? Straight out of Dickens.

~

Skid got married today to a model-turned-copywriter. They met six weeks ago.

~

My father has taken early retirement, bought a 50-foot yacht (having sold the family home last week for a song to my sister Jane) and says he's going to circumnavigate the globe. He's never sailed before, but at least is sensibly taking a couple of crew who have previously ventured beyond the Serpentine.

~

While I was helping my father Tom (he hates me calling him Dad) clear out the house this afternoon, I accidentally hoovered up a large clump of curly dark hair: his keepsake and all that was left of my mother.

~

The old man cast off today from Brighton Marina. Light luggage and a heavy heart. He was married to my mother for 30 years.

~

DDM office party. Lena the hot German has come along as my date (much to my colleagues' amazement) but is spoiling my moment of gloating glory by copping off with one of the other guests right under my schnozzle. I'm not bitter, though; she and Natalie look great together.

~

Skid and Domini are moving to Australia next week. He was born there when my parents became 'Ten Pound Poms' and embarked on a cheap one-way ticket on the good ship Arcadia in the 1950s. My mother said it sucked (women were not allowed in bars in the outback at the time) and came back to London with my infant brother shortly afterwards. It took my father a further two years to save up for his own full-priced return fare.

~

The Psychedelic Furs are the most happening band in the UK at the moment. Tonight I'm experiencing their 'Cacophony of Sound' and 'Beautiful Chaos' at the Lyceum Ballroom in the Strand. I'm completely hypnotised.

~

One of the Psychedelic Furs songs, 'Sister Europe', is the post-punk equivalent of 'Anarchy in the UK', albeit with absurdly obtuse lyrics. The Furs singer Richard Butler looks like the bastard offspring of David Bowie and Johnny Rotten with the attitude to match. The support band was pretty good too. A young Irish four-piece, with a mullet-headed singer called Bono.

~

Today I was made redundant. Apparently there's a recession. Still, a great reference and three months' leaving salary has given me enough dough for a new bass amp and a month's deposit and rent on a top-floor studio flat next to Richmond roundabout. I just need to halt my nights out until I get another job.

~

Well, cut down at least.

~

Gainful employment is proving to be somewhat elusive.

~

I've run out of money, so I've signed on at the Department of Health and Social Security in Richmond. The dole cheque around here is like a grant for aspiring musicians, wannabe actors and jobbing painters and decorators who barely bother to scrape the paint off their boots, overalls and knuckles when they come to the office to declare they have not worked since their last visit.

~

The ad I've placed in *The Melody Maker*, the band-formers' bible, reads:
    Guitarist wanted to join Lady Screen (singer, bass, drums).
    Must love The Psychedelic Furs
    Attitude over ability

Style over substance
Only fringes need apply!

~

'Yeah, I'm ringing about the ad.'

'Great… and you're a Furs type guitarist yeah?'

'Well, I was when I was *in* the Psychedelic Furs.'

Shit, am I really talking to Roger 'Dog' Morris the quiet, quirky rhythm/lead, six-string gunslinger who's just recently been booted out of the Psychedelic Furs? I'm trying to sound cool, but coming across like a star-struck kid phoning Noel Edmund's *Swap Shop*.

'So, erm, Dog, sorry Rog, sorry, I mean Roger. Do you fancy meeting up with us this weekend and we can play you something?'

'Sure, let's meet at the Grey Horse in Kingston on Saturday 1 p.m., see you then.'

'Yeah, that would be…'

He's hung up!

~

It's Saturday. Roger's just strolled nonchalantly in to the pub. I'm with my best mate Colin, an accomplished singer in the Bolan/ Bowie mould, who I first met at a Damned gig, still dressed in his school uniform, astride an actual pogo stick (mimicking the punk rock dance of choice, the Pogo).

Don't act like a fan. Don't act like a fan. Don't act like a fan.

'Hi, Roger. Great to meet you. I'm such a big fan of the Furs.'

Bollocks. Bollocks. Bollocks.

'Really? I'm not,' he deadpans.

~

To his credit, Roger seems to be an incredibly modest guy considering he has just come straight from playing with the coolest band since the Pistols, The Stooges and the MC5 all rolled into one.

~

I'm playing Roger a demo tape of a couple of tracks on my new Sony Walkman, recorded in Colin's parents' living room with Colin on vocals and guitar, me on bass and Julius, a Keith Moon-like friend of Colin's, on drums. He loves it. He's in. I'm assuming it's a rebound situation as, objectively, he's just swapped an Arabian stallion for a one-legged donkey.

~

Roger joining Lady Screen has made up for me not getting the audition with John (Siouxsie and the Banshees) McKay's new band. He said I looked the part, but made Sid Vicious sound like a virtuoso.

~

Our drummer Julius has hooked us up with our first gig, via his old man Dixie's aristo contacts: an 18th birthday party at a stately pile somewhere in the middle of nowhereshire.

'Don't fuck it up,' he tells us encouragingly, as we load Julius' drums into the van. 'I've put my head on the block for you guys.'

~

Our designated driver/roadie is stopping at every petrol station en route to the country for a pee and a hit of amyl nitrite. We've got to the gig earlier than when we left London.

~

The winding drive up to the house from the estate's gates has given us time to take stock of the situation. We have had two band rehearsals. We know five songs. We have all been drinking since lunchtime.

~

The poor innocents, who all look like they are in the waiting room for Oxbridge, are expecting a cabaret band so it's no great surprise that we have completely emptied the room by the middle eight of our first song. Four single barrels gunning down the assembled double barrels, with flange, phase, echo and distortion and that's just on the vocal.

~

We've treated the rest of the gig as a well-paid third rehearsal and indulged ourselves for another 30 minutes. As I get stuck into the post-show birthday spread and some fine wine liberated from its dusty bottle, I can't help but notice there's an altogether different class of totty here than I'm used to seeing down at The Black Dog in Twickenham. It's posh, it's beautiful and it's thoroughly uninterested in me.

~

We're back at Dixie's friend, Candida Lycett Green's imposing country gaff; our designated crash pad for the night. She is both welcoming and accommodating. Her old man, Sir John Betjeman, is our beloved Poet Laureate and Candida has obviously inherited his refined taste. I could seriously get used to this.

~

I've kicked off my Chinese slippers, loosened my 'Count of Monte Cristo' cape and made myself right at home in one of the spare bedrooms allocated to the band, which Colin is convinced is haunted. The only spirit that I can feel, however, is the half-bottle of vodka that I've brought back from the party to help aid restless sleep.

~

My fortnightly dole cheque seems to last me only about three days, so I've solved this monetary shortfall by securing a temporary job at Our Price Records in Putney. I spend all day telling would-be purchasers that we are out of stock of whatever they ask for and use my time more fruitfully, and totally against company policy, recording a huge assortment of mix tapes from the vast selection of records at my disposal. It's only been a couple of weeks and I'm already giving Richard Nixon a run for his money.

~

A postcard from the old man. His round-the-world trip has stalled in Majorca. Storm repairs. He says he loves it there and might stick around for a while.

~

Nine months of every third customer buying The Human League's *Dare* album and Our Price have informed me that my services are no longer required. Apparently, 'You don't want to buy that rubbish!' is not the correct response to a customer asking for the latest ELO release.

~

Lady Screen has split up. Roger has decided to follow his American girlfriend back to Los Angeles. He suggested the band go with him, but Colin is totally loved up with *his* new girlfriend Emily, so I guess that's it.

~

I just had a meeting at Cinderella Rockefeller nightclub in Kingston, on the recommendation of a friend who knows the new manager there. They are looking for someone locally with an 'alternative look' to host a one-off 'alternative dance night'. I'm certainly local and have thoroughly embraced my new crimpers, turquoise Crazy Colour hair dye and the seductively enticing Miss Selfridge make-up counter. I'm hoping I fit the bill.

~

I fit the bill.

~

Cinderella's is looking pretty full, with an interesting array of people. I'm showboating in a hired, sparkly morning suit and full white slap. Rocking the Goth/usher look, I seem to be wearing more make-up than most of the local student girls strutting their stuff to Dead or Alive, Soft Cell and Associates put together. In fact, the only way this warpaint is coming off is with a pickaxe.

~

Not one, but two breakfast companions. Sophie and Sally obviously like their men in mascara but, more likely, couldn't face the journey home all the way back to east London last night.

~

Skid and his wife Domini have had a baby boy, who they have named Lucas after the drummer in Motörhead. Skid's gone back to paste-up and has managed to set up his own below-the-line art studio overlooking Sydney harbour.

~

I started at *London Alternative Magazine* today as a page-layout artist, having answered an ad in its classifieds. For some strange reason I was the only person who responded and even then, all through the interview, they kept calling me Dick.

~

London Alternative Magazine, shortened to *LAM*, is a free Australian weekly focusing on sport, music, sport, film, sport, nightlife, sport, theatre, sport and sport. I hate most sport. At school I was always on the second field with the fat boys and the asthmatics. My gym teacher used to call me Mr Immaculate, as he claimed that my sports kit was cleaner after I came off the football pitch than when I started the game.

~

One apparent perk at *LAM* is the freebies. Concert tickets, records, videos, books… It's like Christmas every day.

~

Donald Mcleod, the *LAM* editor seems a pretty cool bloke, as do the other guys in the art room. I rather gilded the lily about my graphic design course at the London College of Printing at the interview and failed to mention I only turned up about four times. Still, they seem more interested in the next round than my art skills. So here I am, in the pub. It's 5 p.m. Short day then.

~

Still in the pub.

~

My bladder's woken me up. I'm still drunk and my hangover has a hangover. I just looked in the bathroom mirror and my worst fears have been confirmed. It wasn't a dream. I really did shave my eyebrows off at the after-pub party. My head looks like it's on upside down and my mouth's drier than a nun's knickers. I also seem to have misplaced one of my new silver motorbike boots and gained a top hat. There's puke in the toothpaste glass and a girl in my bed. It's 1 p.m. I love my new job.

~

Ten months of page layout, a pint in every pub in London and I have somehow talked Donald into giving me a try-out for the vacant music and nightlife editor position. My only previous writing experience is 500 jaunty words extolling the magnificence of my orange Chopper bike for the local scout magazine, circa 1973, but Don's accepted my career change without any fuss. We have agreed to take the magazine in a cooler, left-field direction.

~

My first piece is on Leigh Bowery and it doesn't get more left-field than that. Leigh's a mad Australian (hence the editorial nod) performance artist/fashion designer, who looks like Henry VIII on shrooms, with his shaved head, polka dot painted face and 'pleased to meet you' webbed body stocking. He's also about seven foot tall in heels, which is just as well, as I'm interviewing him at his home, a council flat on the 11th floor of an East End tower block that you wouldn't want to be in a mile radius of after lights out.

~

Leigh's striking another great pose for the photographer on his triple king-size 'orgy' bed.

'If these walls could talk, darling.'

~

I'm at Taboo at Maximus, a club in Leicester Square run by Leigh Bowery with DJ Jeffrey Hinton. Donald loved the interview and photos, so much so that this week's cover story is Madame Bowery in all his glory. It's a bit of a departure from Aussie Rules football and Leigh has celebrated that fact and rather industriously collected about a hundred copies of the magazine with his smiling mug on it and used them to completely cover the dance floor.

'Makes a change from people *sitting* on my face,' he says, motioning to the hyperactive scrum of arms and legs now turning my prose into pulp.

~

Now as music and nightlife editor, rather like the Queen, I don't need to carry any cash.

'That's fine, Nick, it's on the house.'

'Oh, you're with ten people, no problem.'

'Don't worry, I'll send a car to pick you up.'

I must have accidently skipped M in the careers encyclopaedia.

~

I love getting the latest records to review as I'm rather conveniently situated next door to the Record and Tape Exchange. Promo only not for resale!

'£5 ok, guv?'

~

My intravenous shot of freebies and close relationship with Donald is predictably starting to bug a few of my workmates and the invites to after-work drinks are becoming few and far between, but no worries, tonight it's Astral Flight at the Embassy Club. Nick plus five please. Then on to hear Mark Moore's energetic set at the Mud Club, run by another flamboyant character, the pantomime dame-like Philip Sallon.

~

Much like Boy George, his closest friend, Philip's extremely acerbic and very funny. 'Why use one word when three will suffice?' He has been known to hold up a mirror to the face of a prospective clubber, who he has just refused entry to, and ask them with mock outrage if *they* would let themselves in.

~

To Michael and Gerlinde Kostiff's Kinky Gerlinky club. Androgyny is the order of the night. Hicks with flicks dance with chicks with dicks. Sexual boundaries are not so much redefined as redesigned. I've gone to town with the toner and tongs, yet I still feel like Jon

Voight's character in *Midnight Cowboy* when he arrives wide-eyed and open-mouthed at Viva's party.

~

I have a new favourite group, The Smiths. I've been a little slow to cotton on to their brilliance, but better late than never. To me they represent pop music in its purist form, with a liberal touch of floral stardust sprinkled on top, and are worthy recipients of the T. Rex baton.

~

Colin and I just spent the day watching Live Aid. When Bob Geldof launched the whole Band Aid phenomenon, I rather embarrassed myself by phoning up Bernard Doherty, their media representative, and asking for a press, i.e. complimentary, copy of the *charity* single 'Do They Know It's Christmas?'.

'I think you're rather missing the point, don't you?'

~

An afternoon at Angie Bowie's house interviewing her for a profile piece. Her PA warned me in advance not to ask any questions about David. That's a bit like asking Colonel Sanders not to mention chicken.

~

A quick catch-up with my sister Jane. She's just got back from seeing our old man in Majorca, who now has a Spanish girlfriend two years younger than my sister, who is 27. I was a mistake, hence the age gap. Apparently I came out of the womb wearing my mother's coil like a crown.

~

I tried cocaine for the first time last night, courtesy of one of my ever-expanding circle of plus-ones.

'Do you know you are so beautiful, Lucy, and you, Holly. I've been meaning to tell you that. Have you got another cigarette? Really, have I? Five already? Can I change the music? Oh, I know what we've gotta hear right now. Isn't this track, no, no, track three, track three. Maybe it's track four then. Got any chewing gum? I've always wanted to record a song like this, the strings are like cancelling out all the… everything, and it's just so… Have you seen his new movie? Isn't he the best fucking actor you've seen in your whole life? What's that great scene from his first film? Something about, "If I knew the answer to that madam, I wouldn't be drinking your husband's liquor." Oh I know, she's peerless too, isn't she? Remember that mad play she was in about the Deep South and all the time you're thinking that she's the victim and then it turns out… Shall I get some more wine? Then it turns out… Did he? He's such an unusual guy. Quick, stick on some Abba. Great hair, eh? It's weird, it's like every one of their songs is telling *your* story right, don't you think?'

~

Not a minute's sleep last night, so I'm in Bar Italia in Soho, sipping my third double espresso, desperately trying to survive the day. I'm taking a slash every two minutes and my internal organs won't stop arguing. It's called 'a gram of regret' for good reason. Unfortunately, I cannot really see myself having an early night tonight as I can't bear to miss out on anything. London's the most amazing city on planet Earth and I'm smack bang in the heart of it, though this morning I think I exited through its arse.

~

I called Skid and told him about trying cocaine.

'So we're both snorting shit except mine's from soiled nappies,' he joked.

~

Just got chatting with a wild-looking guy called Ollie Wisdom in a supermarket in Chinatown. He fronts the Goth band Specimen and started the Batcave in Soho. I told him what I do and said I would try and get him a front cover. I'm really starting to sound like a tosser.

~

I've strolled in late today. I'm still piecing the previous evening together. A Durutti Column gig, then on to the Milk Bar? Mod Bar? Mad Bar? Who knows? Donald's away visiting friends in Australia, so my time-keeping's pretty much gone out the window. Everyone's looking really solemn. The receptionist is in tears. The publisher wants a private word in his office.

'I'm afraid I've got some very sad news, Nick. Take a seat. Don got caught in a freak rip tide in Australia and is missing presumed drowned.'

~

I'm sat with Donald's replacement, still grieving.

'You know, Nick, what this magazine really needs is a lot more sport.'

Game over.

~

Skid and Domini have had another son, Julius.

~

With my journo career cut dramatically and tragically short, I've decided to move into club promotion, which I'm told is quite lucrative. An easy and obvious sidestep I figure, as nightlife has been my oxygen since discovering the queue-jumping, dignity- (and quid-) saving 'guest list' and no need to trouble daylight at all from now on.

~

Mandy Miami, another mad Aussie who I met at Donald's wake, has nabbed Thursday nights at Heaven nightclub and wants me to help launch Miami Nights. She's a cartoon version of a cartoon character. Bleached hair, baby-doll dress, massive tits and a toy-boy boyfriend. I love her.

~

Heaven is a cavernous gay nightclub, owned by Richard Branson, set over three floors, tucked behind Charing Cross station. It's shabby and full of cockroaches, but pretty damn cool. The Thursday night slot is traditionally the club's only mixed night and therefore the hardest to fill, though David Inches, the club's manager, seems pretty affable and open to new ideas.

~

The meeting went well. It's been agreed that I will design the flyers, backdrops, etc., and generally help to run and promote Miami Nights. I'm probably the only hetero person here, but well aware that the gay scene is always way ahead stylistically of its straight counterpart, although most of my friends now think I'm batting for the other side.

~

Andy Warhol is coming over to promote his new show at the Anthony D'Offay Gallery and Mandy says we are going to throw a party for him. We are talking about the *same* Andy Warhol, I hope.

~

I've read Andy Warhol's *The Philosophy of Andy Warhol: From A to B and Back Again* and soaked up his advice on anything being achievable: if one, you believe it possible and, two, ignore everybody else's opinion. I'm a huge fan, but can't quite believe that Andy and Mandy are bosom buddies.

~

It was Skid who first turned me on to Warhol and in turn the Velvet Underground, Edie Sedgwick and the whole Factory Superstar scene. Silver became my favourite colour overnight and 'Venus in Furs' self-consciously kicked the Bee Gees 'You Should Be Dancing' off my pubescent playlist.

~

Any doubts I had about Mandy's connections were blown away this morning, when Mandy handed me a 'money can't buy' invite to the Andy Warhol private view at the D'Offay Gallery in a few days. That's me, Andy, a smattering of press and a bunch of rich, potential collectors shooting the shit over a glass of warm red.

~

Not only have the gallery let me in without any fuss, but Andy's signing *all ten* of his Elvis print postcards that I've brought along with me on the off chance. As Warhol, by his own admission, generally gets one of his Factory assistants to silk-screen his work, you're basically just paying for his signature anyway.

'What does that say?' I ask him, pointing to the black squiggle on the last Elvis to get his stamp of authenticity.

'That says "love Andy".'

All without barely moving the contents of his Stephen Sprouse wig. Now by Warhol standards, this is verbal diarrhoea, 'Gee,' being his normal stock response to everything.

~

I can't help but hover by the desk where Andy is sat serenely like the Queen giving her Christmas Day address. Now in spiritual terms, Warhol has always been my Dalai Lama and I'm more than happy to worship at his altar of hype. By contrast, the other guests seem more interested in the art on display.

~

Personally, I've always found the artist more interesting than the art and never more so than in the case of Warhol. It's weird being part of this circus. I keep pinching myself, thinking I'm going to wake up any second, but no, it's all very real… and then, just as quickly as he arrived, Andy and his entourage exit the gallery and head off for dinner.

'I'm afraid it's NFI for us,' Mandy informs me.

'NFI?' I ask, somewhat bemused.

'Not Fucking Invited,' she whispers back.

~

It's party night at Heaven. Andy Warhol's on walkabout. There's a weird fetish act on stage which he seems rather drawn to. It's a huge relief that he's actually shown up, as he's famous for not attending his own parties or sending someone in his place to be Andy for the night. We even traded a couple of 'Gees' in the VIP bar earlier, where I've used Warhol's iconic lip design as the complimentary drink ticket.

~

Most of my friends in attendance are gobsmacked that Andy is here. A few thought it was just a Warhol-themed fancy dress party and have rather embarrassingly turned up dressed as him.

~

Miggy Drummond, a childhood playmate, has just excitedly told me that Andy has agreed to shoot his band Curiosity Killed the Cat's next video in New York. This will turn out to be one of Warhol's last projects, before his unexpected death from complications following a gallbladder operation a few months later.

~

Following Warhol's death (in true Warhol style), I phone up one of the big art auction houses, out of curiosity more than anything else, and ask if they would be interested in seeing/valuing a stack of signed Warhol postcards. They tell me to bring them in. At that moment, I seriously regret having already given away most of my Elvis prints as some very expensive birthday and thank you cards.

~

I arrived at the club early tonight. It stinks of paint fumes. It looks like the main clubroom has been painted purple… and the loos… and the cockroaches. Mandy's in her element.

'It's all very last minute, but it looks like we might be doing a party for Prince.'

~

It's rained every day for the last two months. A friend has offered me £500 for my last Elvis. Time to dig out the mini atlas.

~

The saying goes that all the mad people in the world head to America. All the mad people in America head to California. All the mad people in California head to Los Angeles and all the mad people in Los Angeles head to Venice Beach. I'm in Venice Beach, visiting Roger 'Dog' Morris (who's packed in music and is now restoring antique furniture) and I've just found the place where all the mad people in Venice Beach head to.

~

A stick-thin girl in a blood-spattered Mötley Crüe t-shirt (who claims to have not slept for four days) just joined me in the communal steam room of the hotel where I'm staying, asked me how long I've been dead, then passed me a breakfast bowl full of pinky-white powder, which unfortunately turned to paste quicker than you can say 'pass the straitjacket'.

~

I'm doing all the tacky tourist stuff. The Hollywood walk of fame and sign, the film studio tours, Melrose Avenue, the hills… The problem in LA is that everything is spread over such a wide area compared to London and it's not a great place for pedestrians. People will drive to the end of their drive here, to pick up their car.

~

I can't get over the choice of food that's available or the standard of service in America. I just went for breakfast in a fairly ordinary, street-corner diner and ordered scrambled eggs on toast. By the time the waitress has reeled through the list of different types of bread on offer, they'd stopped serving breakfast and I had to ask for the lunch menu.

~

A final rummage around a funky little record shop before heading home. I've decided on the latest Aerosmith album. The assistant wants to know what format I want it in. Colour vinyl, twin cassette, CD… Sod this, I've got a plane to catch.

~

I'm on my way to LAX, Los Angeles' international airport. The rather rotund Mexican taxi driver, who has stoically picked his nose for the whole journey, wants to know where I am from.

'London.'
'No kidding, I'm going there next year.'
'Which part?'
'Paris.'

~

Observing my black shirt, black Oxfam (dry-cleaned twice) suit combo, the perma-smile woman at the check-in desk has just jokingly asked me if I am going to a funeral.

'Yes, my father's.'

I'm sure it is more out of embarrassment than compassion, but she's upgraded me nevertheless.

'A glass of champagne, Sir?'

'Thank you.'

I'm going to feel really guilty if the old man carks it now.

~

I'm hitchhiking down to Brighton to see Flash for Lulu play at the Escape Club. My driver keeps slumping over the wheel. He says he's been on the go for 24 hours, delivering electrical supplies the length and breadth of the country. I'm desperately trying to keep the conversation flowing to make sure he stays awake. Just another five miles to go and I should hopefully have enough time to get a pint in before the band hit the stage.

~

We've hit the central barrier, done a full 360 degrees and ground to a halt. I miraculously still seem to have all limbs intact and my driver appears pretty nonplussed about writing off his truck, an occupational hazard it appears.

'Cheers, mate. Right here will do fine.'

~

I'm still super-charged from the massive endorphin invasion triggered by the accident. The band sound like they are playing in slow motion and everything seems a tad off kilter. I've definitely used up one of my lives today, so decide to preserve the rest by taking the safe option home: the last train back to London.

~

I once hitch-hiked around a Middle Eastern country on my first solo trip abroad. I'd spent four hours at a dusty intersection with no luck, before a passer-by explained to me that my upturned thumb, a sign I took to be universal, was suggesting to my would-be lift that 'they might like to go fuck themselves'.

~

I've formed another band with Colin, Mardou, named after a character in a Jack Kerouac novel. Our press release and cod call to arms, reads:

MARDOU Embrace the Balls of Byron, the Humour of Kesey, the Front of Ali and the Licks of Ronson, though we know, that we know not what we do.

~

Tonight's our first (and last – musical differences) gig at the Limelight, a new nightclub on the site of a former church in Shaftsbury Avenue, Soho. There's just enough time for a last-minute hair check in the knee-high, broken mirror in the dressing room, which is four floors from the auditorium. I'm wearing a red leather, full length, military jacket, a purple silk tunic and new, heavily tinted, prescription, Cat-style glasses, which are so dark I can barely see my reflection. In fact, I can barely see my nose.

~

I've finally found the backstage entrance, having just got hopelessly lost. As I hurriedly take the stage to the chorus of slow handclaps, I fail to notice the bass monitor next to the drum riser and hit it at full pelt, catapulting myself into the audience in the process. I can hear my wrist snap as I hit something hard, four feet below. The band all think it's hilarious. Not so the girl I've just landed on and knocked out cold.

~

Mandy has gone back to Australia, so Miami Nights is no more, but David Inches has suggested I continue on my own. The new name

I've decided upon is Metro, after the Fritz Lang film, *Metropolis*. I've just got to find a different angle, a fresh theme or, failing that, the same old, same old.

~

The club's filling up slowly tonight. Same old, same old. I am struggling with my new contact lenses. I can't stop winking. One of the barmen has called me over.

'I thought you were straight?'

~

I've given up on the lenses and have settled for clear plastic frames, à la Warhol.

'Chemistry lab cool,' suggests David. 'If that's not an oxymoron.'

~

Metro is plodding along, but it's not the same without Mandy. I miss the madness and feel quite uninspired. Colin, always the voice of reason, reckons I just need to see daylight again, so tomorrow I'm off to visit the old man in Spain for the weekend.

~

Palma Airport. Hand luggage and the obligatory bag of PG Tips for my father Tom. He looks well. Majorca obviously suits him, although Anna, his Spanish fling/fly, is no more. A tough old pepper steak and a quick glass of Rioja in the port and we move on to the Waikiki Bar in Plaza Gomilla. Laval, its Chinese proprietor, puts on Sinatra's 'New York, New York' (my father's favourite song) the second we enter the bar. Tom uses my arrival as an excuse to try out the toxicity of Laval's new cocktail list.

'...and a Mojito, a Whiskey Sour and a spicy Bloody Mary. Right, that should sort me out. What are *you* drinking?'

~

Tom appears to know the whole island. His Spanish vocabulary doesn't stretch beyond 'si', but he can deliver this in a hundred different ways. Twenty-minute conversations with the locals take place with him just nodding.

'Si! Si! Siiiiii!'

'They're probably saying, "I've put all my drinks on your tab, you stupid old bastard",' I tell him.

~

Word of my father's generosity has spread like the crabs that are doing the rounds of Majorca's expat community.

'He got so out of it one night, I swear, *guys* were coming out of here carrying roses,' recalls Ron, an ex-multimillionaire with terminal cancer who lost all his money on 'fast women and slow horses'.

'Well at least I've got my health,' he jokes.

~

Suitably refreshed we head for Tito's, a brand new super-club that has just opened around the corner. One of Tito's imposing walls is made entirely of glass and looks out over the marina. Rumour has it that the lights and lasers had to be stripped out after the first-night party, as they inadvertently started redirecting flights attempting to land at nearby Palma Airport.

~

A quick spin on the dance floor where I'm dancing like my dad, with my dad, and then we stumble to the nearby Don bar to meet David Gosling, a good friend of my father's from London, who is actually two years younger than me, though worldly beyond his years.

~

The Don Gomilla, one of my old man's favourite drinking stops, is owned by a tall, paunchy Brit called Lance, a former British water skiing champion. Lance's mother was the infamous Lady Docker and he jokes with me that when he was growing up he lived above a grocer's.

'Fortnum and fucking Mason, darling.'

~

David's father Donald co-owns NCP Car Parks and is seriously minted, yet David portrays no sign of a silver spoon. He is totally unstuffy and great company (although the school photo in David's loo featuring his old classmate Prince Andrew does at least suggest a certain institutionalised early youth).

~

Back to London and back to work… or not. David Inches has given Metro and me the elbow. It's 1988 and the whole club scene has rapidly changed over the last year or so, helped considerably along by a new recreational drug. Its full name is 3,4-methylenedioxy-N-methamphetamine, so I can understand why it's been shortened to ecstasy or E. It's not actually that new, having first been synthesised in 1912 by a German chemist named Anton Köllisch looking for a substance to prevent abnormal bleeding, but it's certainly new to London. Remarkably, my father has already tried it in Majorca, but I'm yet to indulge.

~

A DJ called Paul Oakenfold has taken over Monday nights at Heaven and called it Spectrum. Similar club nights from Danny Rampling with Shoom and Nicky Holloway's The Trip are spearheading the second summer of love, a new music genre known as acid house and the return of the smiley face logo as everyone's 'getting on it, matey'. The scene's birthplace is the Balearic Islands, so I guess that's why my father beat me to the drop.

~

I'm at my first warehouse party in Vauxhall with Colin. New colourful boho/baggy look, an ever-expanding musical appetite (although my music taste has always been pretty eclectic) and buzzing with ideas. I've definitely got my club mojo back. These illegal all-nighters held in dilapidated abandoned factories (or later, muddy fields, which the media will dub rave culture) are a really refreshing change from my usual haunts, but somewhat lacking in the lavatorial department for someone as anal as myself. Still, the atmosphere is friendly... really friendly... really, really friendly. I guess the E's kicked in then. I'm smiling like a con on release day.

'I feel like fucking Zebedee,' I try telling Colin, but can't quite finish the sentence.

~

I'm levitating. My face has physically frozen into a Gorgonzola grin and I've already taken three layers of skin off my top lip with my metronome tongue. Every snare beat, every subsonic bassline, every choppy piano stab or string run is mainlining straight to my brain. I love Colin. I love the guy selling warm Red Stripe. I love all the people in the queue for the solitary loo. I love the security guy who's just chucked me out for stripping to my undies.

~

It's 15 hours since I took my first E and my eyes still look like someone's shoved a dry, ribbed poker up my shitter.

~

Colin has proposed to his girlfriend Emily. He has asked me to be best man. He's the marrying type, whereas I find it hard to commit to most things as I have a chronically low boredom threshold. We complement each other as friends, though. I encourage him to be irresponsible. He helps me to drop anchor every now and then.

~

I've been going to the Belverdere Arms in Richmond every Sunday. It's a more genteel, less drug-driven night out, where Gilles Peterson, a funky young DJ, drops rare-groove and heavy jazz tracks, now renamed and repackaged as acid jazz.

~

Suitably inspired, I've teamed up with Pierce and Mark, a couple of Richmond boys, had a crash course in DJing and launched Glory Glory Hallelujah Praise Be To Hard Jazz at the Blue Anchor pub in Kew. I can fake it with the DJing, but get busted every time someone asks what the track I'm playing is, as I'm spinning Pierce's tunes blindly.

~

Pierce and Mark are musical purists and keep talking about the 'journey' they are taking with their records. The only 'journey' I'm interested in is the 'journey' back to the cute redhead by the bar, who's just asked me to her place for a nightcap.

~

Skid and Domini have added to their brood with their first girl, Clio. For someone that never wanted kids, Skid's knocking them out at a rate of knots. His finances have shrunk in direct proportion and he's now working 14-hour days to compensate.

~

A phone call out of the blue from an old *London Alternative Magazine* colleague.

'Hi, Nick. I'm now working at *Time Out* magazine and I hear you are out of work, so if you fancy doing page design again, there's a three days a week vacancy going here?'

~

I thought my paste-up days were over, but you don't look a Trojan gift horse in the mouth. It's *Time Out* magazine, an institution that's been the leading guide for entertainment in London since the publisher, Tony Elliott, founded it in 1968.

~

I'm at a pub in Covent Garden with Trish Callahan, the art director of *Time Out*. No real conversation relating to the job has taken place. Instead we are discussing our favourite bands, TV shows, drink… She is lovely.

'So I'll see you next week then, about 10 a.m.'

~

I have settled in nicely, though considering *Time Out* is a magazine about going out 'eight days a week', I'm very surprised to find that most of my colleagues' partying doesn't stretch beyond a few swift ones on the way home from work. The atmosphere is more studious than sybaritic and reminds me of my local library on a wet Wednesday afternoon. On the plus side, the opportunity for misadventure here seems to be as equally open to the art room guys as anyone in editorial, so I have decided to make up for this seemingly lack of serious ligging and go to everything.

~

I just leapt on what I thought was an offer of theatre tickets and inadvertently volunteered my services for a charity bungee jump. The drop's on Wednesday.

~

Bottled it.

~

Every time I mention *Time Out*'s name on the door, I'm told 'Some of your colleagues are already here.' It's never anyone who actually works for *Time Out*. Generally speaking, 30% of the people in attendance at any press event are there for no reason or purpose other than the free booze and the canapés. The rest tend to be freeloaders.

~

A book launch, the opening of a new lighting shop in Notting Hill, a couple of shorts in The Groucho Club, a members' only (and guest... me) establishment for rampaging media types, and then a final thrust to a nearby club for one last drink, where someone pops something dissolvable in my glass. I assume it's one of those fizzy vitamin C tablets that make your pee glow in the dark. Not so. I wake up in the loo a short while later, as a bouncer's boot removes the cubicle door from its hinges and I'm out on the wet pavement.

~

I think I was in the Astoria.

~

I've ended up in Battersea at some famous record producer's riverside pad with a few other wiped-out souls.

~

I think it's Battersea.

~

I've just finished my first feature layout. It looks pretty good. I'm still a dab hand with the old scalpel, even with a bad case of the DTs.

~

I had a kick about at lunchtime with *Time Out*'s five-a-side football team. They said it's just a laugh. They take it very seriously. I lasted 15 minutes and ten of those were waiting in the line to be picked last.

~

My colleagues and various other freelancers here may not all share my social mania, but nevertheless they are an interesting mixed salad. Photographers like Barry J Holmes and Perou, style writer Alix Sharkey and weekly columnist Jon Ronson certainly give my working day some colour.

~

It's Friday and a bank holiday weekend. I'm starting the evening at a new tapas bar in Notting Hill. I've just met a group of French students. It's all very *cordiale*. A challenge. England v France at shots. Tequila!

~

'He's alive!'
   Loud cheering and it's woken me up. O, sweet mercy. It feels like my head's in a clamp. More cheering.
   'Another tequila!'
   Where the fuck am I?
   'Do you remember going home to pick up your passport?'
   '*Passport?*'
   'Do you not remember the ferry crossing?
   '*Ferry crossing?*'
   'Or getting on this train at Calais?'
   '*Calais?*'
   'Don't worry, we'll be in Paris in 30 minutes.'
   '*PARIS?*'

~

I've got about £6 on me and no credit card. I do appear to have a return ferry ticket, but have just had to jump the barrier at Gard du Nord station. One of the students has kindly offered me floor space and a sleeping bag for tonight at least.

~

I've come back from the station loo and can't find my students… or the will to sleep rough in a glamorised Orwellian fantasy.

~

Hot chocolate, a *pain au raisin* and it's straight back to Blighty on the train, via another barrier jump and the late afternoon ferry.

~

Out on the razz again. More tequila. Luckily, this time I've only ended up on Colin's couch in Twickenham.

~

I will never ever, ever, ever touch tequila again. I've seriously tested Colin's easy-going manner. It appears that I got up in the middle of the night and pissed in his wardrobe.

~

My rented studio flat in Richmond is being sold, so I've had to vacate. Luckily, a friend of a friend has fixed me up with a nice bolthole in Cheyne Walk. I just have to look after a fat Labrador called Pirate while the owner is abroad on business for a few months. Now, I hate anything that moults or slobbers, but Chelsea is Chelsea so I gave the owner my dog-loving spiel with great conviction.

~

I let Pirate off the lead and he's attacked the only other dog on the green. Unfortunately, it's a Pekinese owned by a little old lady. Her dog's obviously dead but Pirate won't let go.

~

The vet who put Pirate down said he was on his last legs anyway, whereas the poor Pekinese was in her prime.

~

I'm back on Colin's couch again until I find a new flat. He's taken to locking his wardrobe at night.

~

A new flatshare in Dean Street in Soho, opposite the Coach and Horses, with an old girlfriend who's just kicked out her new boyfriend. We seem to be the only tenants in the block who don't work from home. It's very bijou, totally kitsch and has a communal roof terrace into the bargain. It's also stumbling distance from *Time Out* magazine and within a 100-metre radius you can, if you so desire, check out a West End show, eat Chinese, French, Indian, Lebanese, vegetarian…, catch the latest arthouse movie, down a peppered vodka shot, get a tattoo, get a shave, rock, rave, tango, salsa, get stoned, get spanked, get laid, get even, pick up your local paper and a pint of skimmed and still confess the lot by teatime.

~

Bad news from the old man. He's run out of money and his police pension just about covers his weekly tab at the Waikiki Bar. To make matters worse, his uninsured 50-foot yacht has been reduced to matchsticks by a freak summer storm.

~

I went to a mad club night last night called Ooh Matron! Kinky nurses administering vodka shots from syringes, mainly to each other and in every orifice. Hospital radio tunes. The very best of naff. I'm sure I saw a tanked-up guy getting actual stitches from one of the tranny 'doctors' and another guy showing everyone how he could give himself a blowjob. My mother's father George would turn in his grave. He was so straight that when we visited him as kids he would only let us watch BBC1 and 2 as he thought ITV far too decadent.

~

My father's struck lucky and landed a skipper's job with a very wealthy guy who only uses his £2 million plaything a couple of months of the year; the rest of the time the boat will be at Tom's disposal.

~

Berlin for the weekend. Colin's stag do. We spent the morning checking out all the places where Ziggy and Iggy hung out and recorded and then, in the afternoon, nosed around all the historical sites. Spandau prison took me back to my trainee surveyor days.

~

A relatively tame dining and drinking session last night in a traditional German cellar bar, so on top form today and flowing with the go.

~

Cancel the flow. We've crossed into East Berlin via Checkpoint Charlie and without a doubt we're in the most miserable place I've ever had the misfortune to visit. Everything here feels oppressively monochrome. The restaurant where we have stopped for lunch is serving workhouse gruel with a Stalag side and the waitress has a face like a bulldog licking cat's piss off a stinging nettle.

~

I can clearly understand why so many people have risked, or lost, their lives trying to escape the suffocating existence of communist rule here. Fuck has it made me appreciate my life in London... even more.

~

Colin's wedding is tomorrow. I'm going for a couple of drinks after work, then an early night.

~

My early night unfortunately turned into an early morning at some random after-club party in Bayswater. I'm sure someone spiked my drink as I went from merry to madman in one glass and that was around 7 p.m. Colin says he's heard of the bride not turning up before, but never the best man. At least I've made the reception... well, the end of the reception.

~

I have been dabbling with music again. It's an addiction that will always be with me, though I have swung in a totally different musical direction. My friend John Dowsett, an old schoolmate of Colin's, has bought a high-tech sampler and I've made the most of *Time Out*'s record cupboard and started giving him dance records to fuck around with. The attitude is very punk in that you don't have to be a great musician (you just require a great selection of records to sample).

~

The folksy style songs I've been writing on my first six-string guitar suddenly sound a damn sight cooler when they're dropped over a house or break-beat drum loop. I just need a singer.

~

I've found a singer. My flatmate, wrongly thinking I'm staying away tonight, has let her 'incredibly talented' friend crash in my bed… I've just arrived home. It's 1 a.m.

'Budge up, then.'

~

Harriet Williams is a student from the Guildhall School of Music. A year into a two-year opera course, she also sings soul, jazz and gospel. A posh white girl with a voice like a Memphis mama.

~

We've recorded a couple of songs in a cheap demo studio in Kingston, Surrey. Michael Martin, a young video director (who was looking for a band to shoot for his new show reel), loved the demo I sent him via a mutual friend, so here we are – Harriet, John and me – on a freezing cold morning, shooting a video for 'Feel My Love' in the grounds of Battersea Power Station.

~

The stylist has put John and me in black, boot-cut jeans and Milk Tray polo necks and dressed Harriet like a Victorian doll. Michael has storyboarded the video as a dream sequence, so John and I have spent most of the day gesturing to imaginary people, while Harriet writhes around on the floor looking lost.

~

John's left the band to concentrate on DJing, so the video's out of date before it's even been edited. Luckily, we have a load of backing tracks recorded already, so at least we can crack on with the music side.

~

I just called CBS Music, one of the world's biggest record company.

'Hello, CBS.'

'Yes, can you put me through to A&R please?'

'One second.'

'Diane Jones.'

'Hi there, my name's Nick. I'm in a band called Baseland (named after a 50s pulp novel) and I was hoping we could come and see you and play you some tracks.'

'We don't see unsolicited bands. Send me a tape and I'll give it a listen. Reception will give you the address.'

'Oh dear, that might take too long. We've got a meeting with EMI on Friday, you see.'

'Who are you seeing there?'

I read out the name that I found a few hours earlier in *Music Week*, a trade magazine for the music industry.

'Really. He's back from holiday already?'

'Yeah, he got back today.'

'Well, do you want to come in on Thursday, I've got a 15-minute slot at 5 p.m.?'

~

Harriet and I can barely contain our excitement as we walk through the revolving doors of CBS in Soho Square.

'I hope she hasn't called EMI.'

It doesn't matter if she has. I've already called them myself and done the same scam in reverse. We're seeing them on Monday.

~

Diane Jones looks a lot younger than she sounds on the phone, which is a relief. On goes our demo. Two bars into the song and her phone rings.

'Hello, Diane Jones.'

Her conversation lasts the exact length of the track. Take two. 'Feel My Love' gets its second airing and this time there are no interruptions although Diane does sit in deadly silence for the whole four minutes.

'Anything else to play me?'

I pass her the tape of our latest backing track. Diane pops it into her cassette player and on cue Harriet stands up and belts out the vocal.

'It sounds great, have you many other songs?'

'Loads,' I lie. 'Just not recorded.'

'OK, I'll stick you in the studio next week and we'll take it from there.'

~

Four quickly written and recorded songs later and we're waiting for CBS and EMI's response. I'm planning my stage outfit for *Top of the Pops*, a show I've watched religiously since I was eight years old.

~

Still waiting.

~

Still waiting.

~

I can see now why A&R's are nicknamed Ums&Rs.

~

Both companies have 'passed' on Baseland. *Top of the Pops* is going to have to get by without us.

~

Nothing to lose, so I've sent the tape to Alex Patterson who is Um&R at EG Records, home of Roxy Music and Killing Joke. Alex also has a successful recording career as The Orb, an ambient house duo.

~

Alex loves the demo. He wants to meet up and Youth, his sometime collaborator in The Orb, to produce us.

~

We've just signed to EG Management, although Alex has left EG to concentrate on The Orb after just two meetings with him. Luckily, Pete Smith, another EG employee, loved the demo too and followed through with the deal.

~

Before I put pen to paper on the contract, I've whipped down to the local high street solicitor and changed my surname to Valentine as I think it's a lot more 'pop'. Colin says it's a lot more 'tosspop'. Now as Skid is my only brother and he's now a Marx, I've just ended 700 years of family history.

~

Time Out magazine has let me take a few months off while I see what happens with EG and my new career as a musician/ songwriter, something I've longed for since that first bass guitar lesson with Steve Currie.

~

Mark Fenwick, owner of EG Records, whose family also have the department store chain Fenwicks, has assigned Pete Smith to find us a producer.

~

Pete has teamed us up with Julian Stewart Lindsay, a London-based songwriter/producer and the plan is to record a few tracks for the potential first single. *Top of the Pops* is back in the frame.

~

Courtyard Studios is a residential 24-track studio in Oxon owned by Chris Hufford, who is engineering our session today. He has just played us a demo of a new band called On A Friday that he's going to manage. We discuss shoegazing bands, like Chapterhouse and Slowdive, which Chris engineered, and the American grunge scene. Ironically, Nirvana's epic 'Smells like Teen Spirit' has gone galactic and launched a thousand and one imitations, just as I've hitched my bandwagon to the dance express.

~

Although Baseland are a million miles away from the current rock scene, we have the advantage of a new computer programme called C Lab, that Julian our producer utilises to emulate a 12-piece band, while only having Harriet and I as members and the occasional session musician. No shitty rehearsal rooms, no gigs in pub toilets, no band fallouts, and more importantly, house music is giving me the same epinephrine rush that I first experienced at the momentous Clash gig at the Music Machine in 1978.

~

I went to the local pub The George and Dragon last night with Chris and On A Friday. They had a few A&R guys up from London sniffing around.

~

The sessions are going very well. Julian loves to stop for afternoon tea. It's all very civilised. He's even more anal than me.

'It's the Virgo in us, darling,' he jokes, while patiently recording the eighth take of a three-note piano part.

~

Julian has called in bass maestro Dale Davis and Steve Marsden, the sax player from London-based, urban soul band, D' Influence. I think we've nailed the first single.

~

My father Tom called me today from Spain. He's been given a year to live. Lung cancer.

~

I met Tom and my sister Jane at the hospital. He's come back to England for a second opinion. The consultant has told him nine months… tops. He seems quite philosophical about the situation and, on the surface, quite unaffected but then he's never been one to show much emotion.

~

Skid and I had a pretty lengthy phone conversation about Tom last night. He has always seemed pretty indestructible to us, so we're both in a state of shock. Whereas my brother and I take after our mother, in that we're lovers, not fighters, our old man has always been a bit of a tough nut. I remember him once knocking a family friend out cold with one punch, after he made a disparaging remark about my mother: fighting skills picked up during his time in the Royal Engineer's boxing team, while doing National Service.

~

I've just seen off Tom at the airport. He has gone to Thailand for a 'final fling'. He's been told to stop smoking, a habit picked up at 13, but figures the horse has already bolted. He made a rather shocking confession to me before he left. Apparently, while my mother was pregnant with me he was having a casual affair. He had no idea what his lover did career-wise, until the *midwife* turned up at our flat to deliver his third-born.

~

We're recording a few extra tracks with John Waddell, a far more rough and ready producer, who has cut his remix teeth with De la Soul, Adeva and a lot of the Cool Tempo acts. His afternoon treat is slightly more toxic than Julian's, but lifts the spirits all the same.

~

EG Records now have six finished tracks to choose from. I'm feeling fairly confident and mentally preparing my Brits acceptance speech for Best Dance Act, while practising sucking in my cheeks for the imminent photo shoot.

~

Pete Smith's chosen the first single, 'If They Could See Me Now'. EG just needs to sort out the distribution side.

~

I'm off to La Gomera in the Canary Islands for the weekend. Colin's old flatmate Pony (so-called because he used to design the My Little Pony toys) has been booked to DJ at a Full Moon Party next to a Sannyasin retreat on the beach and suggested I tag along.

~

The Sannyasins are a semi-religious group founded by Bhagwan Shree Rajneesh, otherwise known as Osho, who strive for self-knowledge through meditation yet appear to incorporate a parallel, somewhat hedonistic, lifestyle into their ideology. Detox and retox; sounds right up my street.

~

I've never been a great flyer. I tend to spend the whole journey staring intently at the stewardesses' faces looking for signs of imminent disaster. This flight is somewhat different. I drop a couple of Valium and by the time we hit 30,000 feet I'm already at 40,000 feet and rising. I drift off into a plane crash nightmare and awake suddenly screaming, 'Brace, brace!'

~

I've completely scared the living shit out of everyone on the plane.

~

Valle Gran Rey in La Gomera is only a two-hour ferry ride from Tenerife, but it might as well be another universe. The party is on the outskirts of a sleepy, lush village with unspoilt beaches, Swiss-style chalets and hippies living in caves on 'Pig Beach'. Pony is billed as 'Top London!' so we toast our next ten drinks as 'Top vodka, Top beer, Top rum, Top tequila…'

~

We made the plane journey home with seconds to spare. Top taxi! Though I'm not feeling at all 'Top' right now.

~

EG is still trying to sort out the distribution of our first single through Virgin Records. Richard Branson has just sold Virgin Records to EMI and the ramification is that Baseland are now in a very long queue while all the new administration is being sorted out.

~

The Stones drummer, Charlie Watts, famously said that he'd spent 25 years in rock 'n' roll: 'Five years playing music and 20 years waiting around.'

~

I now know how he feels.

~

Still waiting.

~

Still waiting.

~

I'm not going out at all at the moment. I can't seem to take delight in anything while in this state of limbo and I keep thinking about my father's life ticking away in days.

~

A phone call from Chris Hufford. On A Friday have changed their name to Radiohead and signed, ironically, to EMI. I'm very pleased for Chris. He was having a tough time when On A Friday landed in his lap. In future years, every time Radiohead release another bestselling album, Chris buys the house next door in his terraced street and knocks a hole through the wall.

~

I'm back working at *Time Out* magazine. Still waiting.

~

My father's returned from Thailand and is staying in a hospice in Guildford. Drugged up to the eyeballs on morphine, he barely knows who I am and I certainly don't recognise him. He has lost about four stone in weight and keeps talking about the smiling fish on the next bed in his opiated, delirious state.

~

Tom has refused chemotherapy and is deteriorating by the second. I still remember him at his best, holding court in the Waikiki Bar, everyone around him hanging on his every word.

~

Skid's flown in from Australia and joined my sister Jane and me at Tom's bedside. Likewise, his old friend David Gosling. Various family members drop by over the course of the week. Each of their faces reflects the horror of my father's condition.

~

It's time for Skid to go home to Australia. With three children to support he has to get back to work. My brother has to say goodbye to Tom, knowing that it's the last time he will ever see him alive. They exchange a few last words then Skid leaves, only to return a few minutes later and repeat his farewells all over again. He eventually says his final goodbye and I can't look him in the eye. My father seems pretty oblivious to the mass of sorrow surrounding his bed.

~

David and my sister have gone back to his for a freshen-up. I'm chatting with Tom but the conversation is only going one way. I have to keep sponging out his mouth as his lungs seem to be breaking up into sticky, spongy globules.

~

Shit. Tom's body just shuddered from head to toe. It's like he's been plugged into the national grid. He's growling in a terrible, unearthly way.

~

Another twisting jolt.

~

Silence.

~

It's all over.

~

I continue the one-sided conversation with Tom for another hour or so, before finally informing the nurse that my father is dead.

~

In one of Tom's last lucid moments, I asked him who he would like to come back as, in a next life.

'Me… I'd come back as me,' he replied.

~

I can't quite believe that my father has gone. When the phone rings I freakishly think it's going to be him on the other end. I have Frank Sinatra's *Songs for Swinging Lovers* on repeat play and family photos spread all over my bed. I don't remember my mother's death affecting me in quite the same way, although I have known my father for ten years longer and wrongly assumed he was indestructible.

~

My sister and I spent today going through Tom's personal effects. In the end his life's possessions fitted into one battered suitcase. His estate totalled £20 and that was the money I gave him for ginger beers from the soft drink machine at the hospice. He always said you can't take it with you and he was surely true to his word.

~

I've finally given up on EG Management/Records. Baseland is no more. All the waiting around has killed our spirit and the one feeling my father's death has galvanised in me is to not waste any time in life and try and maximise every day. A cliché, I know, but death is a great catalyst for clichés.

~

Time Out is switching to computerised design. I can stay and train up on the new system (I'm a Luddite to the core) or buy a one-way ticket to Thailand.

~

Charlie Loucke is the Far East correspondent for an Australian broadsheet, who I first met while travelling around Egypt. A perk of the job is his five-bedroom mansion in the centre of Bangkok, complete with a chef, housekeeper, gardener and chauffer. He has kindly offered me one of his guest rooms as a stepping stone on my way to the islands.

~

A contemplative breakfast in the sun. Last night Charlie took me to nearby Patpong, which my travel guide describes rather innocently as a 'landmark for evening fun' and Charlie more brutally as 'a Disneyland for pervs'. On the first floor of a three-storey building that gets wilder as you ascend each flight, a middle-aged Thai woman removed a string of razorblades from her Jack and Danny. Charlie, who covered the Khmer Rouge atrocities in Cambodia, bailed after the second floor.

'You don't wanna know,' was all he could manage, before suggesting we head back home to watch *The Antiques Roadshow* on satellite with some tea and biccies.

~

I've hooked up with an old friend, Andy Hobsbawm, son of the renowned Marxist professor Eric, for the trip south. The boat from Surat Thani to Ko Samui was a living nightmare. I was seasick all the way and Andy had his wallet lifted. The bucket of Sang Song and coke has done the trick, though, and we're right back on track, although I do feel like I've just pickled my innards.

~

The Reggae Bar is bustling with an eclectic mix of travellers, hookers, expats and lady boys, or 'katoeys' as the Thais tenderly describe their cross-dressing national treasures. It's quite unbelievable the amount of pissed tourists who happily leave on a promise with no clue as to the meat and two veg about to be served up to them.

~

Koh Pha Ngan is a ravers' paradise. We are here for tonight's world-famous Full Moon Party. Your credibility here is measured by how little you pay for anything. Andy and I have out-cooled the coolest. With our late arrival on party island, the only accommodation that we've been able to find is a storage cupboard: no windows, no loo, 40 baht between the two of us.

~

I've managed to score a couple of disco biscuits (500 baht, bang goes the beach cred) and jumped right on the 150 bpm. It's mental. Two hundred up-for-it people, pumping music and a gentle, cooling sea breeze: the perfect combination. The E's very trippy and I keep seeing movement from the corpses of the feral dogs that were culled earlier today by the locals and discarded at the foot of the beach.

~

The boat that returned Andy to the mainland and relative sanity has delivered my next travelling companion. Pete Cattaneo is a

Twickenham boy, who I was briefly in a band with (three rehearsals, no gigs). He is now a fledgling film director and is travelling around Asia before he starts work on his first feature film, a low-budget, Sheffield-set comedy about a group of unemployed steel workers who become male strippers. Fast forward a few years and it will go on general release as *The Full Monty* and become one of the biggest-grossing British films of all time.

~

We've hired a jeep and set off for a remote beach resort on the Malaysian border, leaving behind my holiday fling Jenny, a Welsh beauty who works for Saatchi and Saatchi and would give an impotent corpse a hard-on.

~

The locals told us earlier we can walk through the sea to a nearby uninhabited island. They failed to mention you can only do this in the morning before the tide turns. It's 2 p.m. Pete has disappeared from view. I can no longer feel sand beneath my feet. It makes no difference, if I try to swim ashore or to the island, I seem to be stuck between the two. I'm utterly exhausted and there's not a soul in sight.

~

I've been trying to stay afloat for an hour or so now and have resigned myself to the fact that I'm going to drown. I'm a devout atheist who has been praying to someone/something for the last ten minutes, making promises I will never keep. I feel surprisingly calm. I'm thinking maybe Tom's getting lonely already and wondering what song I would like played at my funeral. I can't decide between 'You Can't Put Your Arms Around a Memory' by Johnny Thunders or the Paul Anka version of 'My Way'.

~

Both my legs have given in to cramp. It's just my rapidly fading arms barely keeping my head above water. I'm swallowing mouth after mouth of sea water and my lungs feel like they are about to burst. This is it. Lights out…

~

A Thai fishing boat has materialised from nowhere. It took three of my lifesavers to pull me into the boat. I'm in too much of a state of shock to thank them when they deposit me ashore. Pete's rocked up oblivious to my close shave with death, but has alarmingly pointed out that I'm slate grey in colour.

~

Johnny Thunders nudged it by a smidgen.

~

Just touched down in Sydney. I have decided to pay my brother Skid a surprise visit. Unfortunately it's the evening of Australia Day and I can't get a cab for love nor money and stupidly have lost Skid's phone number but, thankfully, I at least have his address. It takes me as long to get to his house in Manley, mostly on foot, as it did to fly in from Thailand.

~

I've woken up surprisingly early after yesterday's ordeal. It's time to meet my nephews and niece for the first time. Skid's wife Domini is pregnant again and at the puking stage. For someone with OCD, Skid's keeping his sanity remarkably intact considering all the toys and general kiddie mess that's cluttering up his apartment. He says he copes with it by storing all his worldly possessions in one, locked, immaculate cupboard.

~

My body clock's still a bit fucked up, so Skid and I have headed out for a revitalising breakfast of coffee and more coffee by the Sydney Opera House. He is now making a living doing silk-screened portraits of Australian celebrities à la Warhol and tells me that paste-up, as in England, is on the way out in Australia.

~

Suitably charged, we've decided to head up the coast and stop en route at an ill-famed barren headland, where those of a mad disposition can jump from the top of the cliff into the relatively shallow water below. Skid's done it once before and says the buzz is like doing ten espressos in one hit. Madness prevails.

~

The X-ray confirms I have a cracked coccyx.

~

If feels like I've just spent a week on the segregation wing of a South American prison having loudly asked, 'Who fancies some loving?' I have to sit on two plump pillows on the flight back to London, much to the annoyance of the guy behind me who wants to watch the in-flight movies.

~

Back in England. My father's good friend David Gosling, who I bonded with over a crate of San Miguel in Majorca, has rescued me from living in the style I don't want to get accustomed to by offering a rather grand roof over my head. I'm not to the manor born, but certainly to the manor drawn and, boy, is David's gaff a mother of a manor. This recently purchased pile in Godalming, a renovated old farmhouse set in a couple of hundred acres of deer forest with a man-made trout lake, is a bit of a step up from my last flatshare and only a 50-minute journey to Waterloo Station on the express train.

~

My new room is minimal, has a pleasantly, pastoral view and is set away from David and his girlfriend in the west wing. I've started making a list of potential sleepovers.

~

We celebrate my arrival with a few bottles of wine. David suggests a quick scuba lesson in the safe environs of the outdoor swimming pool. It's freezing. I'm hammered. I come to the surface too soon. In just seven foot of water, I manage to blow an eardrum. From now on, any new musical venture is going to be strictly in mono.

~

Having failed miserably in the aquatic stakes, David figures I might be suited to more traditional country pursuits. He loads a shotgun for me. I've never fired a gun before. I aim and try and shoot the runaway clay. The recoil nearly takes my shoulder off. We try quad biking. I write off the bike and my left ankle. Fishing; hook in my cheek. David is slowly and meticulously maiming me. He says I've taken to country life 'like a duck to a pancake'.

~

I spent the day on the phone trying to drum up some work. So far, so bad.

~

David and I have found a nice quiet spot by the lake to plant a cypress tree and scatter my father's ashes in its roots. With my sister Jane and her two-year-old daughter Holly in attendance, we carefully lower the tree and ashes into the hole we have meticulously dug. Just as we all close our eyes and contemplate Tom's life and death, Holly rocks forward and falls face first in to the ashes. She emerges tearfully, her face contorted, slowly spitting the remains of my father out of her mouth.

'I guess Tom's ashes are going to be spread a little further afield than we imagined.'

~

I reckon I'm going to have to move back to London. I'm out every night partying/networking/looking for work and never seem to manage the trek back home to the country and there's only so many times you can turn your pants and socks inside out.

~

I think I got offered a job last night. Now if I could only remember who offered it and what the job was.

~

Skid and Domini have had another boy… Piers.

~

I've moved in with Martin Dunkerton, an old mate from Teddington who is both easy company and huge-hearted. It's a tiny basement flat, but has a great south-facing garden and the rent is cheap. Situated on the W10/W11 border, house prices shoot up with every paving stone south, whereas due north your chances of having your face mashed in increase with every tentative step. We are right next to one of the most notorious drug-dealing streets in the borough and every fifth building appears to accommodate a crack house. A consequence of this is an ever-constant police presence and enough closed-circuit cameras on my new doorstep to make Big Brother seem discreet.

~

Martin is a film graduate from the Royal Academy of Arts and is into all things mystical. He has rather kindly feng shui'ed my

room for me. Aromatherapy and crystal cleansing follow. Finally,
I'm asked to pick a medicine card. It's a rabbit, which explains the
colour of my aura apparently. He calls everyone matey and I've
started unconsciously mimicking this.

~

I asked matey, I mean Martin, why the woman who he's writing his
latest 'nuclear proliferation' script with never drops in for a cuppa.

'Because she's been dead for ten years, matey. I'm just her
medium.'

~

I'm settling in nicely. Last night I slunk around the corner from my
new abode to see the Stereo MCs play at the Tabernacle church.
On the way home I ran into Joey Ducane, a local singer/songwriter
out on the town with 60s icon Anita Pallenberg. I asked Anita who
her favourite rock star of all time was and she told me country rock
legend Gram Parsons, which is rather surprising as she has had well-
documented relationships/flings with The Rolling Stones' Brian
Jones and Mick Jagger and a son, Marlon, with Keith Richards.

~

I just had an interesting interview with Robin Duff, a Kiwi
journalist in her mid-40s, who I met briefly at some launch or other
when I was at *Time Out* magazine. She is boffin-smart, bursting
with energy and the proud proprietor of *London At Large*, a new
entertainment press agency run from a couple of windowless box
rooms in Marylebone.

~

When Robin and I were first introduced a couple of years ago we
hit it off immediately, both sharing a blacker than black sense of
humour, and she suggested I get in touch with her if ever I was
at a loose end workwise. I guess unemployed and broke is a pretty

loose end.

~

'You know the entire London party crowd. You're out every night anyway. If you come and work here, you can have the rock 'n' roll lifestyle, without having to bother with the rock 'n' roll.'

~

On a scale of 1 to 10 for the perfect job, this is hovering around an 11.

~

The sales guy, an acne-scarred court jester in a demob suit, was in the middle of being sacked when I arrived at Robin's office this morning, so I've slunk next door into editorial. Caroline Citrin, the Scottish, prohibition-dry editor of *London At Large* has coyly passed me the *LAL* manifesto, a ten-page ramble outlining the thinking of my new employee. Great, a fruitcake at home, a fruit loop at work.

~

Robin fills me in with the workings of the agency. Simply put, *LAL* gathers information on future entertainment events – film premières, restaurant openings, album launches, art exhibitions, product promotions, celebrity appearances, fashion shows – collates it into a diary and flogs it on to newspapers, magazines, broadcast media, PR companies, photo agencies and whoever else can afford the subscription fee.

~

I've just popped over to the launch of Channel 4's new season in their swanky offices. Robin's told me to 'network', which I interpret as stuffing my face full of cold salmon, knocking back a barrel-load of sweet white and giving out my new social editor business card to anyone with a pulse.

~

This 'networking' malarkey is easier than breathing for me, as I'm happy to shoot the breeze with almost anyone. Robin, by contrast, has an almost phobic hatred of bores and thinks nothing of wandering off mid-conversation if someone fails to amuse her. We certainly make an interesting party duo.

~

I spent the day contacting every PR company in London to make sure I'm on their invite radar. I've just got to sit back now and wait for the pitter-patter of not-so-tiny envelopes to arrive.

~

You can generally tell the quality of nosh you're going to be served at an event by the thickness of the invitation. Photocopied or flimsy and it's straight in the bin. Gold trim, rounded corners and the obvious attention of a fine calligrapher; skip lunch and blag yourself an extra invite.

~

The launch of Una-Mary Parker's latest blockbuster at the Ritz falls into the must-attend category. My threads are more clubby than couture but I'm still rather taken aback that a well-known female thespian has dragged her bony old frame off a nearby chaise longue just to ask me if I came in via the backdoor.

~

My unready-to-wear problem has been remedied by a good friend who works for Nicole Farhi and I'm now the proud leaseholder of a beautiful pin-striped, forest green, velvet suit.

~

It's not unusual to have eight or nine different press events in one evening, so your freeloading has to be planned with military precision. It's a highly skilled art form just knowing in what order to attend the night's festivities.

~

I'm debating with Robin whether we got it right *starting* at the party (in a grungy old warehouse in Hammersmith that's been transmogrified with thousands of candles, cushions and billowing drapes) to celebrate the opening of Donna Karan's new London flagship store.

~

A film première bash at County Hall is a great excuse to nose around Ken Livingstone's former office. It's a convoluted maze but a sharp left and a quick right and I've ended up in front of the feted showbiz hymen that is *the velvet rope*. This restraining instrument of social apartheid is there to keep the Ps from the VIPs. To a serious partygoer like my dear self, it has the same allure as the last jump at Aintree to a thoroughbred.

~

After a punishing amount of deferential banter, the penguin-suited obstacle, whose sole job all evening is to be as obnoxiously rude or sickeningly sycophantic as your VIP status dictates, has finally lifted the rope. I'm in. Ten swaggering steps later, the champagne on offer has turned to warm wine and everyone around me looks a little bit on the P side. Yes, it's quickly dawned on me… I was already in VIP and have just blagged my way *out* of the area.

~

I'm at the launch of a nightclub called the Aquarium in Old Street.

I've somehow ended up naked in the pool with a couple of helium balloons tied around my todger. Oh look, there's Mick Hucknall.

~

I was so wrecked when I left the party last night, the winos around Old Street station avoided making eye contact with me.

~

I'm at Atomic Model at Iceni nightclub. French Marc, the managing director, hosts the VIP third floor where the likes of Sylvester Stallone, Jack Nicholson, Tom Cruise, Bryan Adams and Bruce Willis come to party. Because of a lack of floor space and keen to maximise the take, Marc has opted for the relatively new profit-pusher in UK club land: the minimum spend table. In addition to the usual club staple of champagne on offer, Marc has brazenly added magnums of various spirits at £200-plus a pop to the menu. Just for the exalted privilege of sitting down, you have to guarantee a minimum drop of up to £1,000 depending on the size and positioning of your table. By prosaic contrast, I'm stood bolt upright at the end of the bar, next to the gents, nursing a glass of warm beer… but still loving every second of it.

~

The British Academy's Film and Television Awards (Baftas) are the closest we come to matching America for celebrity glitz. This ceremony is our considerably less star-infested equivalent of the Oscars, but still a prime invite for the budding salonista. I'm strolling down the red carpet with a *seriously* hot date on my arm. As we squeeze past John Travolta to get to our seats, I notice that my supremely cool companion is rapidly defrosting. I scan the brochure that has been given to every guest and stop at the seating and status plan. Yep, there he is, John Travolta, Chris Evans, Kylie Minogue… Nick Valentine (NO DINNER).

~

As harsh as it is being brutally reminded of my place in the pecking order, I'm still milking every party for what it's worth, particularly on the date front. My love life has definitely increased pro rata to the amount of velvet ropes I'm now breezing past.

~

I've just arrived at an old school hall for the launch of Boy George's autobiography, *Take It Like A Man*. The party has a St Trinian's theme and George, dressed as a corduroy-jacketed sociology professor, complete with food-ingrained beard and patchwork trousers, has managed to stay completely incognito all night, as guests ponder his no-show.

~

I didn't make it home last night, so I had to take the Tube to work this morning still dressed as William Brown from *Just William*. The girl whose flat I ended up back at told me she had 'never done this before'.

'What, a one-night stand?' I enquired.

'No... a guy,' she responded. 'But I think I'll stick to girls in future.'

~

Back to my old stomping ground, Heaven, for Fraser Clark's Megatripolis, a festival within a club, with a progressive house, trance and ambient musical policy. It's a kaleidoscopic mix of eco warriors, ravers, poets, musicians, performance artists, cyber punks, old hippies and blissed-out new beatniks. A bit like a weekend stroll down Camden High Street, really.

~

A David Bowie private view with the *artist* in attendance is an invitation I gleefully snapped up. I'm a huge, huge fan, though his recent body of music hasn't exactly set the airwaves alight, so I figure a career change is probably a wise move. I figured wrong. I pass a mesmerised critic who is staring intently at one of Bowie's *creations*.

'He's so brave, so brave, don't you think?'

'What, turning up?' I ask, just as the former David Jones shuffles past us and out of the door.

~

Louis Vuitton's *Concours d'Elégance* is another situation where you can view classics of their time that have gone a little rusty. This definitive car competition is held every year at the Hurlingham Club, a private sports and social club for well-heeled members, nestled alongside the banks of the Thames in Fulham. It runs throughout the day, provides lunch and afternoon tea and then slips up a gear at 7 p.m. when the majority of celebs arrive for a sit-down dinner and the chance to relive their youths on the mini funfair.

~

I'm revelling in the novelty of daylight and relishing the thought of a lie-in tomorrow, while checking out a beautiful array of luxurious vintage cars. My appreciation of all things motoring is purely on an aesthetic level. I had my one and only driving lesson on my 16th birthday and, after a fairly major collision just off the A316, my instructor and I quickly and painfully agreed that I make a better passenger.

~

Quentin Crisp, England's finest raconteur and serial party hopper, once professed to living on a diet of champagne and peanuts. I'm exactly the same, except I don't like peanuts.

~

In as much as cruising the canapé circuit means that you never have to place a step inside Tesco, it also saves a lot of legwork when it comes to Christmas shopping. At every single event there's always a 'Thank you for coming' sugar cube. These goodie bags can range from a couple of promo pens and stickers at a low-key and low-budget do to the hamper from heaven at a charity blowout along the lines of Elton John's yearly fundraiser at his mansion in Windsor.

~

Perfume launches are a particularly good source of festive offerings. I quite often, rather than having to carry whatever sweetener I've just picked up (particularly if I've nabbed two goodie bags), give it to a bemused tramp or a grateful cabbie.

'Thanks a lot, mate, my girlfriend will love that. You got another one I can give the wife?'

~

In a typical year hundreds of new venues open and close. There are only a finite number of punters and as London becomes overrun with new bars, clubs and restaurants, so do the Samaritans' phone lines with calls from suicidal City investors.

~

Of course, some restaurateurs still have the Midas touch. The launch of *übermeister* Terence Conran's Mezzo in London's Wardour Street has all the pomp and ceremony of a high-profile film première. Partially clad starlets run the red-carpeted gauntlet of flashing camera lights, heavy security and screaming hordes and that's just to pick up their tickets from the party organiser.

~

The Atlantic Bar, a huge, art deco restaurant/bar in the bowels of the Regent Palace Hotel is the embodiment of the recent gentrification of a lot of old, decaying leisure sites. Oliver Peyton, the visionary behind the project, burst on to the scene when he introduced Absolut Vodka to the capital and spearheaded the London bar trade's move into upmarket, premium brands, a trend that consequently spread throughout the UK, the repercussions of which surround us and lubricate us to this day.

~

Soho House, a new private members' club for film, media and creative types has opened to rival The Groucho Club and already has a waiting list for membership. Tonight, for once, I'm the plus-one, courtesy of my flatmate Martin. I'm wearing three days of stubble, a new two-button, olive green whistle with a matching Agnes B shirt and mock croc Chelsea boots, so feeling quite 'the dandy'. Martin thinks I look like a suburban hairdresser on a stag night.

~

Establishments like the Hanover Grand, the End and the Emporium have sprung up overnight, with interiors that look as if they've been modelled on uptown recording studios or a rock star's weekend palazzo. It doesn't seem that long ago that you'd have to get a tetanus jab before visiting a nightclub's powder room.

~

Bar culture has also undergone a major facelift. Out with spit-and-sawdust and themed pubs and in with New York-style designer bar/restaurants with zillion pound makeovers, modern European menus, mixologists (barmen who know what to leave out of a drink) and in-house DJs.

~

I'm off to the launch of a new music award ceremony, the MOBOs (Music of Black Origin Awards). That's practically every music genre known to man, then.

~

I have an encyclopaedic knowledge of blues music, the result of sharing a bedroom and record player with Skid until I was 12 years old. He has recently capitalised on his passion, started a new band playing harmonica and saxophone and is touring the biker bars and festivals around Sydney. His Chicago blues trio come on between the female mud wrestling and the wet t-shirt competition. Classy.

~

Colin loves new technology. He's an IT manager at London Underground and they've given him a company mobile phone. It doesn't seem very mobile to me. It's the size of a brick and twice as heavy.

~

I've swung by the revamped and relaunched Café de Paris. It's just had a two million quid facelift and looks like it. The VIP rooms have a sunken bath, circular beds and loo doors that are not cropped short at the bottom, as in most London clubs: quite important I'm told, if you fancy a bonk or a bump.

~

A cheeky line of Charlie and I'm now talking absolute bollocks to some giant, flat-nosed, rockabilly dude outside the VIP loos. He's leaned in to whisper something… Fucking hell. He just tried to tongue me.
    'Taxi!'

~

I've just fled back to my flat, tried to pay the cab driver and realised that my wallet has been nicked, so I guess the predatory hillbilly wasn't being quite as amorous as I thought. More like a loving mugging.

~

A late-night phone call from Skid. He and his wife Domini have split up.

~

The media is kissing its own 'Cool Britannia' arse at the moment. A lazy, current soundbite to lump the best of British creative talent in an easily exportable, homogenised package. Pulp *are* the dog's danglers though.

~

Back to the Café de Paris for an exhibition of Rolling Stone Ronnie Wood's paintings, organised by our mutual friend David Morris, the Café's VIP host. Ronnie is actually a really talented artist, as well as being an extremely funny storyteller, but then when you've been in the Stones for as long as he has you're not exactly going to be short of stories, even excluding the ones you have to take to the grave.

~

David's invited me along as his plus-one to Ronnie's Wild West-themed birthday party at his house in Kingston Hill tonight. I've spent a couple of hours in the fancy dress shop and settled on an American Civil War union officer look, complete with a forage cap, sack coat, leather brogans and a fake Colt revolver. I'm just waiting for David's driver to pick me up.

~

An apologetic text from David blowing me out. Bollocks. Not only am I home alone and no doubt missing a monumental party, I'm dressed as Colonel fucking Custer and I've just locked myself out of the flat.

~

It turns out that my coquettish neighbour, who I luckily left a spare key with, loves a man in uniform, so I'm back this evening for round two, dressed as a sailor without a ship.

~

I've been offered a weekend club night at my local watering hole, The Mas Café, by Henry Besant, its amiable manager. This works out well as the press/media/launch scene runs Monday to Thursday and it's fun to be back blagging behind the DJ decks again.

~

The Mas is on the old site of the Mangrove Restaurant where the Notting Hill Carnival office was located for a short while and is the perfect venue for Take My Cherry, featuring DJ Pony and my 'Soulful, Retro Grooves and Free Funk'. Pony's words, not mine.

~

Our launch night is a complete roadblock (largely helped by a noteworthy preview piece from my old *Time Out* colleague, clubs editor Dave Swindells), with the queue starting in Westbourne Park Road. Unfortunately, one of the local crackheads has just done a smash 'n' grab with the cashbox, before Frank, our Rastafarian doorman, could nail him, so with the flyers still to be paid for we've made about minus £150 tonight and our cashier has a black eye the size of Neptune. Monetary and medical matters aside, though, Henry has agreed to make Take My Cherry weekly.

~

Our cashier, not unsurprisingly, hasn't turned up tonight, so guess who's in the hot seat?

~

Pony's set particularly appeals to the local stoners, who all seem to be using the DJ booth as a giant rolling mat. By the time I've fumbled through the fog to split the night's takings with him, I'm too wasted to do the calculation.

~

The ever-increasing frivolity at Take My Cherry has attracted the attention of the local constabulary, who have rather unsportingly shut down our night.

~

Second drugs bust in a week. I'm with Colin on a rare night out from his domestic bliss at Browns nightclub, a celebrity-stuffed party palace. Jake Panayiotou and his brother practically invented clubbing as we know it today when they opened their doors back in 1985. As the police roll in, in ever greater numbers, London's hell-raising hierarchy make for the door, leaving a confetti trail of wraps in their wake.

~

Waste not, want not.

~

Robin says I look like I haven't slept in two days and she's spot on. This must be one of the only jobs where excessive partying is actively encouraged and all I have to do is trade Bellini banter and make a mental note of any upcoming launches, etc. I'm told about that aren't already on *London At Large*'s radar.

'Well, I hope you picked up lots of leads.'

'Well, if that's what they call wraps Down Under.'

~

To the opening of The Met Bar, a new, tiny, members' only oasis in the confines of the partly Robert De Niro-owned Metropolitan Hotel. It reminds me of an airport lounge, though with the heavyweight names behind it, it will almost certainly become a serious celebrity sanctuary. Membership is so exclusive that people are already booking rooms in the hotel just so they can share Martini space at the bar with any visiting A-list star.

~

Back home at the nuthouse, Martin has ditched the ghostwriting and started on a screenplay, loosely based on our collective lads' holidays in the Greek islands over the years, but centred on Martin and his brother Julian's relationship. Julian owns a string of clothing shops called Cult Clothing and, unlike his brother, is more into totty than tarot.

~

I've found myself co-writing the script with Martin, partly so my version of events gets an airing. The working title has stuck and it's now officially called *Brothers*. This is going to be cathartic. I drink to forget. Martin doesn't drink to remember.

~

Martin's a fitness fanatic. He's suggested I join his local health club, Lambton Place. The gym part I'm not really enthusiastic about. However, the pool, the Jacuzzi and the Notting Hill yoga babes that Martin assures me are in abundance swing it for me.

~

I just had my fitness assessed by one of the on-site personal trainers. Considering I'm asthmatic, regularly party beyond the call of duty-free and have not participated in any form of physical exercise since leaving secondary school, I'm amazed to be told I'm in pretty good shape.

~

An indulging, post-swim soak in the mixed communal Jacuzzi. I'm on my tod but hoping one of the Lambton ladies, currently totting up lengths in the pool, may soon join me. The trouble is I can't see further than the end of my nose without my glasses (which I've ditched as they keep steaming up), so unless one of the girls actually sits on my lap, it's going to be hard to tell if she is hot or not.

~

Oh, lovely. Here comes a tall blonde… I think.
    'How you doing?' I ask, as she plops down next to me.
    'I'm alright, thanks.'
    Good God, it may be blonde, but it's also hairy and male.

~

Rob 'the blonde' it turns out, is thinking of moving to the area, so we shoot the breeze about the highs and lows of the 'hood. He's actually quite a laugh.

~

I'm back in the changing room, fully dressed now, with my specs back on. Rob's leaving.
    'Good luck with the house hunt, mate,' I say, quickly realising that I've just experienced what a million screaming teenage girls would give their right arm for… a Jacuzzi with Robbie Williams.

~

I spent the day with an incredibly patient Martin, trying to get to grips with a new concept called Hotmail.

~

The night of the Mas Café bust I got talking to a cool bloke who looks after a chain of clubs and bars in central London. He asked me if I knew any good salsa DJs, as he was looking for someone to fill a vacant slot at Bar Cuba in Kensington.

'Yeah, me,' I replied.

'Really, how long have you been DJing salsa music?'

'About two… three,' I told him, nonchalantly.

Two… three wasn't exactly a lie, if you count it as minutes, rather than years.

~

My new salsa aficionado amigo has just called me to chase my 'show tape'. I told him I've just got to add a few more killer tunes and then I will drop it round. I've just found out the largest distributor of salsa music in the UK, so will give them a call.

~

'Hi, yeah, I'm starting a brand new salsa night at Bar Cuba in Kensington and wondered if you'd like to sponsor the night. You can drape some banners at the club and of course we'll stick your logo on the flyers. All I need in return is some of your latest product.'

~

I'm three months into my run at Bar Cuba. I don't think I can bear to hear another salsa track. It's even seeped into my dreams/ nightmares. I've started playing reggae and Latin jazz instead. No one seems to notice the difference. It's time to hang up the headphones.

~

To Rik Mayall's birthday party with Caroline, *London At Large*'s editor. It's an aquatic-themed evening, so I've come as a lobster. I'm feeling a little out of salts, so a quick face-stuff, a raucous singalonga Elvis session with Rocky Horror creator Richard O'Brien, a slow smooch to 'Lady In Red' with a fit mermaid and I'm ready to head for open seas and home. Caroline says she wants to meet for breakfast tomorrow to run something by me.

~

I'm in Paul's Café in Marylebone, struggling to keep my bacon sarnie down. Caroline's on her third Camel in 15 minutes and she doesn't even smoke.

'How do you fancy setting up our own agency? Between us we've got all bases sorted. I can run all the office-based stuff and you cover the social side. I know a guy called Robert Barclay who owns a company called Profile that puts out a similar thing to *London At Large*, but for the advertising industry, and I think they'd go for it.'

'Fuck it, why not.'

'What do you think of *Entertainment News* as a working title?'

'Well, it does what it says on the box.'

~

Profile have agreed to fund *Entertainment News*, though want to retain ownership and pay us as consultants, albeit double the amount we are both earning at *London At Large*. We move into their offices in three weeks.

~

Robin took the news of our departure surprisingly well and even graciously wished us the best of luck with our new venture.

~

I'm sat at my new desk at *Entertainment News*. We're based in a funky, spacious, industrial block in Farringdon. The atmosphere, however, is as stiff as Casanova's cock on Valentine's Day. Robin may have been eccentric, but at least she created a buzzy, energetic working environment. I'm swapping 'Have we made a huge mistake?' grimaces with Caroline every few minutes.

~

Robert's got a few bottles of plonk in for after-work welcoming drinks. Maybe we just need to shake things up a bit?

~

I might have shaken a bit too hard. I find a drunken game of Truth or Dare always gets the party started… and, in my case, ends it.

~

Now, where did I leave my wallet/house-keys/socks/mind at the house party that a few of my new colleagues ended up at?

~

The atmosphere is definitely less stiff today.

~

I'm calling all my contacts with our new details. The general response is pretty positive. The Profile Group has seven publications in total and a staff of 50-plus. *Entertainment News* has a corner of the open plan office, two telephones, a couple of computers, a fax machine and a few wonky shelves. We've pretty much been told just to get on with it. The launch date is scheduled to be in four months. Heads down, here we go.

~

I've come up with an add-on to *Entertainment News* in the shape of *Red Pages*, a celebrity/PR contacts database, with a published hard copy which we can flog.

~

Three different high-profile celebrities have met their maker in this last month alone. *Red Pages* is rapidly turning in to *Dead Pages*.

~

Four months of 12-hour days, a couple of new suits and we're ready to launch.

~

We've signed up our first subscriber: *OK! Magazine*.

~

Lunch with Tom Parker Bowles. He is helping his cousin Ben Elliot set up a new concierge service called Quintessentially and may use some of the *Entertainment News* content. He has kindly pointed out to me that you don't actually de-shell soft-shell crab.

~

An evening in with Martin working on the *Brothers* script. We're both coming from two totally different places with our creative input, but somehow miraculously weaving it all together. Whether or not it's working is yet to be decided and certainly not by us.

~

To the opening of Home House (formerly the Courtauld Institute of Art), a lavish 18th-century, Robert Adam-designed townhouse turned private club/bar/restaurant/spa/hotel. This imposing property was once the London residence of the infamous Soviet spy Anthony Blunt and now home to anyone with a shitload of cash to throw at the yearly membership fee. That's a shitload more than I would pay to be a member anywhere.

~

Dinner with Colin at Teatro, another members' only bar with adjoining restaurant in Shaftesbury Avenue, which offers an ultra-calm staging post in an otherwise frantic strip. This celebration of muted tones is owned by *Men Behaving Badly* star Leslie Ash and her former Leeds striker hubby, Lee Chapman. Tonight's cabaret is the hip-shaking, spit-dribbling Elephant Elvis, who murders the King's finest tunes in the style of the Elephant Man and, as a grand finale, whips off his hood to reveal a deformed John Merrick-like head, complete with giant quiff.

~

It's sensory treats like Elephant Elvis that keep my imagination and enthusiasm perpetually stoked. Just when I think I've experienced every form of entertainment possible and started to tire of the latest hotspot, someone, somewhere, comes up with a new twist on an old theme and once again I feel like a kid in a candy store.

~

A breakfast meeting with Nicky Haslam, the renowned interior designer. This latter-day Peter Pan, in his late 50s, has reinvented himself with some street threads and a splodge of hair dye as a Liam Gallagher lookalike. He's been on the party treadmill longer than canapés and literally knows or knew *everyone* across all social spectrums, from Marlene Dietrich to Cilla Black. He is looking for a spectacular venue to hold his 60th birthday party, so I have suggested 1 Lombard Street restaurant, a former banking hall, with a neoclassical interior and a Pietro Agostini domed skylight, owned by Soren Jessen, a Danish friend of mine.

~

One of Soren's best mates is Prince Frederick, the future king of

Denmark, who looks (in a positive way) like he would be more at home playing bass in an acid jazz band, than sat on the throne of a tiny kingdom.

~

When I first met Soren I took him and Frederick to what I'd billed as 'the most happening club in London, full of the most happening people'. I phoned ahead to confirm the guest list and explain the security situation. When we arrived later that evening they'd cleared out all 'the most happening people' for 'our benefit' and we were confronted with a completely empty space.

~

I've managed to get Nicky sponsorship from *OK! Magazine* to pay for part of his party. He has faxed me over his guest list, which reads like a *haut monde* who's who and spans three generations of front cover fodder.

~

Payment from celebrity magazines is based on an amount per celeb head, a kind of modern day bounty hunt. In this instance, *OK!* are hoping for at least 30 faces recognisable to their readership.

~

It's party night. Nicky has more than delivered the specified 30, with a plethora of twinkling stars to spare. A Beatle, a Stone, a diva, a prince and plenty of queens. There are semi-naked go-go boys gyrating on the revolving bar and Kate Moss is throwing shapes on the basement dance floor, all under the mindful scrutiny of Soren, who says it's the best event he's ever had at his venue. I feel like I've nodded off and woken up in a Fellini movie.

~

Skid has flown in to deliver the likeness of Nicky that I commissioned for his birthday and cannot believe the amount of potential clients for his portraits within schmoozing distance of our table. More, in fact, than in the whole of Australia and New Zealand put together.

~

News from Down Under is pretty dire. Skid's ex-wife Domini has had to undergo a double mastectomy for breast cancer.

~

At the launch of a new whisky with Skid. He just bumped in to Ron Jeremy, the world-famous porn star, in the loo. I tell him that he has just crossed swords with someone who has fucked more women than Bill Wyman and full fat chocolate put together.

~

To the airport with Skid. I'm really going to miss him. Even if he wasn't my brother, I still think we would be best mates. This trip has made him realise how much he would like to move back to England sometime in the next few years, when his kids are a bit older.

~

The *Brothers* script is finally finished. To be fair, it's a bit of a hotchpotch but Martin's brother Julian, who's made a lot of dough in the rag trade, has agreed to part-fund a five-week shoot in Greece.

~

I'm in Paros in the Greek islands for three days doing some (hmm) research. Martin, meanwhile, is shooting a five-minute pilot to raise further funds, with Bournemouth substituting as Greece.

He's found an upcoming actor called Paul Bettany to play him.

~

The pilot has actually turned out rather well and on the back of it Martin has miraculously raised another £200,000. He has decided to shoot *Brothers* on Super 16 and use a cast of unknowns, who will happily work for peanuts to facilitate their 15 minutes of fame. Filming is scheduled for August, so I can take five weeks' holiday from *Entertainment News*.

~

The budget is now up to £750,000, so we're going to shoot on 35 mm. Investors' contributions have ranged from Martin's brother Julian's £400,000 to friends and family taking a £1,000 punt.

~

As the self-appointed casting director of *Brothers*, I've set about the task with a maniacal passion. This basically involves me asking any animated character that I meet on my nightly jaunts if they can act: if they are female and single, so much the better. There's no harm in it being an enjoyable shoot.

~

Paul Bettany has dropped out and been replaced by another young newcomer.

~

As Driftwood (one of the 'brothers', who all have pet names conjured up by Martin) is based on yours truly, I have the surreal job of casting someone to play me. Martin has suggested I play myself, though I'll still have to do a screen test for the investors, as my last theatrical outing was as Simeon in the St Mary's and Peter's school nativity play, aged eight. I can actually still remember my lines.

~

I called Skid today and he brought the weirdness of the situation home to me.

'If you don't get the part, it means that someone's better at playing you than you are.'

~

I got the part.

~

Heathrow Airport. Here we go. Full respect to Martin for persevering with such a seat-of-the-pants odyssey and Julian and co. for emptying their pockets and funding such a mad project.

~

After a near-mutiny last night over who of the 54 crew and cast are sharing rooms, I've finally settled into my single crib on the magical Greek island of Paros. As co-writer, co-producer and actor, there has to be a few perks and having your own room is one of them.

~

Today is the first day of a five-week shoot and scene one involves me walking along the dock reciting my song lyrics, while I await the arrival of the other 'brothers'. The enormity of our undertaking has just hit me like a sugar-coated sucker punch. Whatever happens with the film now pales in to insignificance alongside the fact that we are actually making it. Crew, cast, location… lights, camera, action, the whole brain-numbing shaboogle.

'And cut.'

~

Filming is, to say the least, chaotic. Ten-ton crew trucks parked on collapsing cesspits. Beach bars charging exorbitant amounts to turn off their music for sound recording. Lead characters hit by motorbikes. Half the crew and cast copping off with each other… and we're only on day two.

~

Bust-ups between Martin and me have become a daily occurrence, spirituality head to head with actuality. His gentle manner conceals, when it comes to work, a kind of stubbornness and blind, striving will that makes Genghis Khan look like a wallflower. Today's 'angel card' pinned on the hotel reception noticeboard for 'inspiration' is Tranquillity. Cue another blazing row.

~

The crew aren't letting any of the on-set bickering spoil their enjoyment. And why would they? We are on an idyllic Greek island during its busiest month. Most days they work a 14-hour day, start drinking the second they down tools, party most of the night, grab a couple of hours' sleep and arrive back on set and ready for action by 7 a.m.

~

Today's my sex scene; a spoof of one of my favourite films, *Betty Blue*, that requires me to simulate shagging a young French beauty. The wardrobe mistress has been sent off to find a flesh-coloured cloth to cover my cock. Suitably wrapped, I start my gyrations. A couple of sweaty takes later and Richard, the director of photography, has halted proceedings.

'It's no good, you're gonna have to lose the cloth, it's still in shot.'

~

I've now got my crown jewels tucked back between my legs. By take five, it feels like George Best has kicked me in the nuts and I've done irreversible damage to the pecker and hangers. Where's a body double when you need one?

~

A big party scene on the beach. Paying and plying the extras with booze turns out to be celluloid gold, but hasn't endeared us to the local dignitaries, who have dropped by the shoot to check that we are portraying the island in a good light, only to be confronted with the kind of drunken carnage that would make Caligula flinch.

~

A rare day off chilling on the nearby island of Antiparos. A warm sea and a cold beer. For all the daily moans and groans from the cast and crew, we all collectively agree that there's certainly worse ways to make a living.

~

I just narrowly avoided decapitation. The scene where I'm standing up on the back seat of a speeding, open-topped jeep didn't take into account any low-slung tree branches overhanging the coastal road.

~

Some of the rushes have come back and after a lot of scrutiny, I've been told that I'm not quite as wooden as I feared.

'But I don't think Al Pacino will be losing any sleep.'

~

I've lost track of what is reality and what is scripted. I asked the waiter at breakfast if he needed to shoot me from another angle after he plopped my Full English on the table. At least I've learned the Greek word for fuck-face.

~

Another day, another drama. Five reels of film have gone missing and consequently we need to redo a whole two-day sequence and bring an actor back to the island, who only headed home to the UK yesterday. He probably hasn't even unpacked yet.

~

Miraculously, we've reached the final day of filming. A few catch-up shots and we're done. It's a wrap!

~

With the footage safely in the can, Martin has somehow procured the talents of one of the industry's top film editors, who is based at Pinewood Studios. He has also got clearance to use Blur's 'Song 2' for the opening titles for a nominal fee and Angelic's 'It's My Turn' for the closing credits.

~

Not being one to let a golden opportunity pass me by, I've written a song called 'Redemption' for the film, using the vocal talents of the elegantly wasted Ollie from the band Freeloader, which runs in its entirety over a segment where a sleep-walking Wildman relieves himself over a sleeping Tarzan.

~

Off to Pinewood Studios with Martin's brother Julian to see the rough cut of *Brothers*. It looks a little bit too cosmic and touchy-feely for my taste and Martin's character, unsurprisingly, rather dominates screen time.

~

I just had a look around the colossal set for the latest James Bond movie, which is being partly shot at Pinewood. It's put our relatively low-budget labour of love into prospective and I'm now feeling really guilty about being so hard on Martin. The truth is neither of us is really happy with the final cut and with hindsight I realise that there were 'too many cooks' on the film and I was almost certainly the one surplus to requirements.

~

A test screening of *Brothers*. Very mixed reactions. An equal number of whoops and walkouts. My performance is thoroughly average at best and that's pushing it, so it's with a certain relief I can now safely cross off acting as a possible new career.

~

A distributor for our, ahem, 'masterpiece' is proving illusive.

~

Martin's girlfriend Joanna, a co-producer on the film, has pulled a massive rabbit out of the hat and persuaded a private investor to finance UK distribution for *Brothers* and, on top of this, has secured a Leicester Square première.

~

Shopping in the King's Road. A new outfit for my special night.

~

I'm with Colin at the première, a screening for 300 people at the Odeon Leicester Square. Black pony-skin trousers and a tight white t-shirt. *What* was I thinking?

~

Pre-screening speeches from Martin, Joanna and the cat's

mother, lots of back-slapping and we're off... lights down. I'm unfortunately sat next to someone, who, oblivious to my role in the film, spends the whole 96 minutes telling his companion in an exaggerated stage whisper what a piece of crap it is. He's so convincing in his delivery that by the halfway mark I'm joining in. He even high-fives me when the lights come up.

~

Post mortem and post-première drinks at the after-party at Soho House. A quick touch-up in the loo and I'm ready for my adoring public.

'Oh, really, you were in it? Which one were you then?'

'Driftwood.'

'No, I don't remember *him*.'

~

With the exception of a couple of lads' mags, one of which has made *Brothers* Film of the Month, the reviews are universally awful. One longstanding television presenter has actually described it as the worst film he has ever had to critique.

~

My skin has grown at least an inch thicker during the course of a further avalanche of vitriolic reviews.

'Well, at least the film's getting a reaction,' I tell Martin.

~

Brothers has transferred to DVD after a short two-week cinema run. I've ventured in to Blockbuster as, weirdly, they have advance copies ahead of us, complete with the obligatory extras.

'You don't wanna rent that, mate,' responds the young slacker behind the counter in answer to my request. 'It's full of benders.'

He is certainly not the first person to comment on the homoerotic undertones of seven sweaty guys bonding in the land of Socrates. Maybe our mini drama has a market after all.

~

Back in the unreal world at *Entertainment News*. I'm looking forward to the launch of a new members' club called China White tonight. It's been described to me as a faux-oriental den of iniquity with a VIP room and chill-out area on raised beds. Somewhat of a one-stop shop.

~

The rise of mass-market members' only clubs, as opposed to established drinking holes like The Groucho Club, means you can now lease a fragment of the ubiquitous velvet rope with your annual membership subscription. Johnny Come Lately has cottoned on to this phenomenon and realised that the poky broom cupboard in his damp, windowless basement can be easily transformed in to *the* latest members' only club.

'We're keeping membership to a cool core 50.' (In case everyone turns up at once.)

~

Space is certainly not a problem for Home, a new cutting-edge nightclub over a multitude of floors in Leicester Square. It boasts an impressive DJ line-up that includes Paul Oakenfold and a VIP bar with spectacular views over London. I am at the launch party sat next to the not-so-cutting-edge Rod Stewart, though I have to confess to being a fan… not to him, of course.

~

Off to the launch of the Titanic Bar and Restaurant, one of super-chef Marco Pierre White's many establishments. Its fate unfortunately is in the name.

~

A shot, shower and a shave and I'm ready for *Tatler* magazine's 'Little Black Book Party' at Mr Chow's restaurant. This is a yearly event celebrating posh eligibles, some of whom will be in attendance tonight, and packs a great goody bag. I'm the first to arrive. I've never bought in to the whole fashionably late syndrome. I like to get to a party early and see what unfolds. Among these blue-blooded singletons, I kind of feel like a roadie backstage at Live Aid.

~

It's home time. I've bumped in to Hannibal Reitano, an Argentinian fellow party addict, who I see at practically every event I attend. He often jokes that he's never done a day's work in his life, but has obviously inherited a wad as he's offered to drop me near my flat in his new Rolls Royce Corniche convertible. As we cruise through Soho with the roof down, *The Best of Disco II* blasting out from his CD player, we are aurally accosted with two shouts of 'wanker' and a token 'knobhead' before we hit the open road. This starts a fit of uncontrollable laughter for both of us and nearly results in Hannibal totalling his new ride, before he's even put double figures on the clock.

~

The Bulgari party for its new perfume. A sit-down dinner to launch Ian (Studio 54) Schrager's St Martins Lane Hotel. A meet and greet with Shania Twain. A charity performance of *Miss Saigon*. The Saint bar opening. The Chelsea Flower Show. The Sugar Reef restaurant launch. The Tate Modern Funding Gala. The Fabric nightclub opening. The Tiffany Xmas bash. The Claudia Schiffer fitness video launch party. The Annual *GQ* Awards. The Serpentine Summer Party. The Channel 5 launch. The Olivier Awards. Brown's Photographic Studio launch. The Club Volante opening. Ascot. The *Vogue* Gold party. The Dorchester Club relaunch. The Puff Daddy album playback party. The private George Michael gig. The *Friends* TV show video launch. The Sotheby's soirée. The *Condé Nast Traveller* magazine drinks party. The Naomi Campbell book launch. The *Evening Standard* Film Awards. The Dali exhibition. The Armani store opening. The *Elle* Style Awards. The L'Odeon restaurant opening. The Gumball Rally party. The For Your Eyes Only club launch. *The Blue Room* first-night party. The opening of Denim bar. The London Restaurant Awards. The Interno 8 Party. The Red Cross Ball. The Agent Provocateur bash. The Land Speed Record launch. The 10 Rooms nightclub opening. The China House launch party. A Ricky Martin shindig and the Mirabelle restaurant launch, all whizz by in a Martini blur. I'm shaken *and* stirred.

~

A good film première and its after-show party is one event that can slow you down for the evening, as you obviously have to sit relatively still for the 100-odd minutes of screen time and then nearly always want to stay put for the extravaganza that follows.

~

Tonight I'm at the première party for *Batman and Robin* at Battersea Power Station. Last week I rather overindulged, canapé-wise, at a couple of parties and managed to get a bad case of food poisoning... a *really* bad case of food poisoning. I suddenly found myself gulping down oxygen in a speeding ambulance and then in a hospital bed with a tube protruding from *every* orifice and I mean every orifice. Up to the point of insertion I'd always thought that a catheter was a light liqueur.

~

A whole week of nil by mouth has done wonders for my cheek bones, so it is with an exaggerated pout that I approach the mélée outside the party entrance, still a little shaky from my drip removal. There appear to be three different queues, depending on the colour of your wristband. These Nazi-like brandings are the civilian equivalent of military stripes and act as your temporary visa into impolite society. I hold up my wrist and, much to my surprise, I'm waved past gold, silver and poop brown. I know the girl who is in charge of sending out the invites, but not *that* well. As I stroll past a vague acquaintance in the main room he grabs my arm.

'Fuck, how did you manage to get Super VIP,' he stammers, tugging on my hospital wristband.

~

Getting VIPs to attend your event is essential. It's their smiling mugs that assure you of column inches and the reason these events have such astronomically large budgets. There are a couple of companies in London whose sole job is to pull the stars from the skies or, failing that, any minor celeb with something to plug who will happily sing for their supper.

~

More often than not, journalists are promised Keith Richards and delivered Keith Chegwin, guaranteed the cast of *Friends* and given the cast of *Hollyoaks*. One company, to their credit, make a very good living out of always supplying the same celebs, namely the blonde one out of a defunct girl band and a male ex-soap star who will go to the opening of a window. Not quite the Oscars, but in the land of the blind the one-eyed celeb supplier is queen.

~

In as much as London has followed the example of its LA leaders and gone celebrity-gaga, it has streaked ahead with its very own version of fame by association. At the launch of a space-age bar in the West End, I overhear the sister of the friend of the wife of the rock star give the 'don't you know who I am?' speech.

~

One celebrity who is top of every party-thrower's hit list is Madonna. I met her very briefly once at the launch of Mourad Mazouz's Momo restaurant. This crushingly chic Moroccan eatery, with a painfully hip basement bar, launched with a sit-down dinner. Fortunately, I was one of the chosen few invited to attend. Unfortunately, Madonna had decided to throw her own even more exclusive soirée in the basement that very same evening. After waiting for my food to arrive for what seemed an eternity and getting drunker by the second, I decided I'd nip downstairs and see if old Madge and her pals were causing the delay. I popped in to the loo first for a quick pee and got chatting to a guy at the urinal, who said he was, true or not, Madonna's feng shui advisor. As he strolled past the hired muscle, guarding Miss Ciccone's privacy, I kept him talking and joined the celestial chancel by default. I've never been one to gatecrash but the rumbling in my stomach was getting more audible and there was, as I'd expected, plenty of nosh on offer. There couldn't have been more than about 30 guests there: Gwyneth Paltrow, Jimmy Nail, Nellee Hooper, the record producer, and a few other bods, but no sign of Madonna. I sat myself down next to a middle-aged woman on one of the North African sofas and tucked into the nosebag.

'So, how do you know Madonna?' I slurred, making civil conversation as much as anything else.

It then suddenly dawned on me who I was talking to, just as Madonna's security arrived and sent me hastily packing back upstairs to the mortals.

~

Skid's finally seen the copy of *Brothers* I sent him.

'Well, at least you got a free holiday.'

~

Martin has decided to add an extension to his flat with an estimated four-month build, so it's time to move on. Our friendship has never fully recovered from the whole *Brothers* debacle, which is a great shame really, though I'm sure time apart will heal any lingering resentments. To give him his due, Martin is pretty tenacious and has already started on the screenplay for *Sisters* without the hindrance of a thorn in his side, namely me.

~

Conner Reeves, a singer/songwriter friend of mine, has rented me his spare room in a very cool loft apartment in St Saviours Wharf in Bermondsey. It's so close to the waterfront that if you jump off the balcony you land in the Thames. Conner had a Top 10 hit with 'My Father's Son' and has written other tunes for the likes of Tina Turner and Will Downing. In all my life I've never seen someone so dedicated to their craft. As a practising Buddhist, his morning starts with a chant and a prayer. He then shuts himself in his home studio and does not emerge until he's knocked out yet another opus.

~

I've started t'ai chi classes. I figure I need a bit of balance in my life. My instructor Jamie Bloom is also one of the owners of the Café de Paris, among many other bars and clubs, so I guess he's on the same trip, but a million miles further down the road. I studied a staff form of kung fu when I was 13 and had an unhealthy Bruce Lee obsession, but can only remember the greeting bow and subsequent battering I received.

'How long does it take to learn?' I ask Jamie, at the end of my first lesson.

'All your life.'

'And if I come *twice* as much?'

'Even longer.'

~

T'ai chi aside, Jamie has asked me to help organise the Café de Paris' New Year's Eve party. I've suggested the idea of a celebration of icons who have misbehaved over the centuries and have decided to go as the prince of degenerates, Lord George Gordon Byron, who famously wrote, 'Man, being reasonable, must get drunk; the best of life is but intoxication.'

~

It's New Year's Eve. I'm kitted out as Byron, looking good, feeling fine, right into character. I'm greeting guests with a nonchalant nod, an air kiss and a dainty flick of my lacy cuff.

'Oh, you've come as Charles Dickens,' states the first cute girl I try and swoop on.

~

The kind of bad behaviour celebrated by our New Year's knees-up has been championed right across the media for a few years now, in particular with magazines like *Loaded*, which sprang up with a cod lad outlook and which suddenly made it socially acceptable for men to get off their tits and the average girl in the street to get out her tits. They essentially took a traditional top-shelf title like *Playboy*, added some drugs and rock 'n' roll and migrated down a shelf or two. It's as punk rock had been many years earlier, a middle class invention for the working class masses, and a very successful one at that.

~

Club impresario Peter Stringfellow has capitalised on this 'new laddism' with the relaunch of his fading 80s eponymous club, Stringfellows, as a table-dancing venue. This is an establishment where a scantily clad, high-heeled girl dances precariously over your seated form, plops her baps and bootie out and then is rewarded with your soggy £20 note for her troubles.

~

Stringfellow, it has to be said, has reinvented the strip joint extremely well with his freshly named Cabaret of Angels and trumpeted in a rush of copycat ventures. I've popped by tonight with a rather flamboyant 80s pop star, who I met earlier this evening at a restaurant launch. Peter, more than a little surprised by my companion's attendance, has asked us to join him at his table. Copious amounts of complimentary drinks and dancing vouchers are generously supplied by our somewhat bemused host.

'I could have sworn he was gay, but he jumped at the chance of coming here,' I whisper to Peter, as my new beer buddy disappears under yet another engulfing cleavage.

~

Conner's moved his girlfriend in, so I've found a flatshare in Earls Court. My new flatmate Sarah designs children's wear for a living and apparently is an excellent cook. She wants to know when I'm moving the rest of my stuff in.

'This is it.'

'You're joking. Are you on the run?'

~

I went to London socialite Andy Wong's Chinese New Year's party earlier this evening. It's 2 a.m. and I'm completely blotto, dressed as a Chinese emperor with a theatrical handlebar moustache. I can't remember my door number, the houses in Redcliffe Gardens all look the same and Sarah's not answering her phone. Cue shouts from passing cars of 'Fuck me, it's Fu Manchu.'

~

I'm meeting Colin and a few of his jazz dance classmates for a couple of drinks at the Minty bar in Old Compton Street. I've just made my way over to a corner table where he's sat in full *Flash Dance* get-up.

'Hi, this is—'

BANG!!

~

Colin didn't quite get my name out before the bomb in the Admiral Duncan pub two doors down exploded. It's utter carnage. Smoke and debris everywhere. Sirens and screaming. A middle-aged guy covered in blood keeps shouting out that there's a second bomb. Panic and utter disbelief on everyone's faces. I'm holding my bag in front of my face, waiting for the second blast, frozen to the spot. Colin's grabbed my arm and dragged me out on to the street. It's like a scene from the Blitz, though this is not old black and white war footage, this is London 1999.

~

We have somehow ended up in Marble Arch. Neither Colin or I can remember walking here, trance-like, though I do vaguely remember the police hurriedly directing people up what I think was Dean Street. We are both in a state of absolute shock. The enormity of what has just happened does not sink in until we eventually get home and see the BBC newsflash.

~

A right-wing extremist has been arrested in connection with the pub bombing. Tragically, two people have died and many others have suffered horrific injuries.

~

Every time a car backfires or a door slams I'm jumping out of my skin. I can't help but think that I will carry this feeling to the grave. Fortunately, I am one of the lucky ones and still alive to write about it, though I've worked out that I probably passed the front of the Admiral Duncan no more than ten seconds before the bomb detonated.

~

I've cut my days at *Entertainment News* down to three a week so I can work on a few other projects. Through a friend's recommendation, I've been offered the chance to do the press and PR for the Inns of Court Ball, an annual charity dinner and dance for the legal profession, held in spectacular surroundings and described as 'Glastonbury in a tux'. The ball's organiser, Jonathan Rich, is a complete laugh despite his conservative attire, and possesses a razor-sharp wit and a tremendous passion for live music.

~

Jonathan's still not secured a headline act, so I've suggested that I try and talk my friend Tony James, of London SS and Generation X fame, into reforming Sigue Sigue Sputnik for one night only. Sputnik burned brave and bright in the early 80s with their space-age blend of cyberpunk and rockabilly and shot to Number 1 with 'Love Missile F1-11', before going the way of most rockets. They have always had a hate/hate relationship with the press, so I figure they are the perfect provocative act to generate some tabloid coverage.

~

Sputnik are up for it.

~

Tony and co., surprisingly, went down a storm and were even relatively well behaved. I've managed, with a little bit of help, to make it through the night to the survivors' breakfast and even cop off with a cute criminal lawyer. I'm sniffing like a Peruvian playboy, so my new companion has suggested we go back to hers for a Lemsip.

~

I attended an interesting dinner tonight. I was sat next to Duran Duran's Nick Rhodes. Meeting him triggered memories of dancing to 'Girls on Film' at some dodgy New Romantic night in a Kingston wine bar in the early 80s, with my purple Ali Baba trousers tucked in to my socks.

~

Queen's drummer Roger Taylor is another down-to-earth guy with an out-of-this-world lifestyle. I first met him at a party at David Gosling's while I was still living there and have bumped in to him from time to time ever since. Tonight I'm off to the Pharmacy restaurant with Roger and an old friend of his.

~

Brit artist Damien Hirst part-owns Pharmacy and has supplied all the pharmaceutical art within, which is worth about ten times the value of the restaurant itself. I'm thinking if I nicked just one of the pill pots, I could probably take it easy for a few years workwise.

~

Roger has asked me to help organise his end-of-solo-tour party. Queen are well known for hosting the most decadent and debauched parties of all time and urban myth has it that at one extravaganza a group of dwarfs were hired to walk around with silver plates topped with mounds of cocaine on their heads, so it's no easy gig.

~

Roger's after-show bash at the Mayfair Club, a new table-dancing venue just off Berkeley Square, is in full swing. There's plenty of eye candy on show tonight and he seems pretty cheery about how things are going. My date for this evening just tripped on the stairs and sent one of her gel bra inserts into orbit. It's now continuing its journey across the dance floor stuck to the stiletto of an unaware reveller, with my mortified date in hot pursuit.

~

Beauty Spy, a new internet fashion and luxury goods site, have agreed to pay me to photograph celebrity guests at the parties I attend for *Entertainment News*, for their social page *Eye Spy*. They also want me to write a bit of blurb to go with the photos. The only catch is that I have to write it in character as a 21-year-old girl.

~

My flatmate Sarah can't understand why I suddenly need to know her dress size and the brand name of her favourite lipstick.

~

I took a few shots of Paul McCartney, Lulu and Britney Spears tonight. It made me pretty uncomfortable as I felt a bit like a stalking fan.

~

My sister Jane has had a mini-stroke. She's only 42, but has sadly inherited a family blood-clotting condition which catastrophically resulted in my mother going blind a year before she died.

~

Beauty Spy has gone the way of a lot of new internet sites that are springing up like distant relatives at a will reading. I'm more than happy to hang up my camera.

~

At the launch of a new sports bar tonight. I've been joking around with an Australian glamour model for most of the evening. She is stark labia naked apart from the sports bar logo, which has been deftly painted all over curvy body. She is up for coming back to mine, but I'm struggling with the thought of all that paint rubbing off on my new whistle in the taxi.

~

Off to meet Colin for lunch. Just need to drop by the dry cleaners.

~

Soren Jessen has asked me to help out with the launch of Noble Rot, a new Nicky Haslam-designed private members' club/ restaurant he is opening in Maddox Street. It has a 1930s Happy Valley/safari theme and is situated over two floors in the heart of Mayfair. A bit of 'White Mischief'. I'm sure I can manage that.

~

New club, new clobber. I'm thinking a flared, three-button suit with a Nehru collar.

~

My flatmate Sarah is getting married and needs her spare room back, so I've jumped at the chance to flat-sit a penthouse riverside apartment in Putney for a friend who has been posted to Brazil for a year. There are obviously substantial perks to being a sugar trader.

~

A fleeting visit to my new local alehouse. I've just been introduced to the confectioner in residence, who for the sake of propriety, I'll call Allsorts. He is far from the usual archetype, being as he is in his late 50s, well-to-do and, I'm told, pretty punctual. Allsorts describes himself as a purveyor of quality treats – uppers, downers, all arounders – and tells me an amusing story about one of his customers, known as Jigsaw, who has an inspired way of stopping himself from sniffing all of his party (cheaper in bulk) four-pack in one go. When he gets his gear, he puts the four individual wraps into four mini combination safes and writes the code number of each safe on the back of a complete jigsaw, which he then breaks apart. The goods can then only be retrieved when the puzzle has been solved. The more complicated the jigsaw, the longer the time between toots. Apparently Jigsaw used to be called Tampon, but that's a whole other story.

~

I'm admiring my empty glass at a fetish-themed party at Papa Gaio, a licentious velvet den buried in the back streets of Soho. One of the members of our kinky-clad group has suggested that we move on to drinking schnapps.

~

Jesus, my backside hurts.

'Who the fuck are you?'

'Very funny.'

'No, seriously, who are you?'

'Err, Alice.'

At least I'm at home, but have no idea how I got here or who my rubber-clad bed companion is. It feels like I've sat on a hot plate and I've got deep welts all over my arse cheeks.

'Sorry I think I got a bit carried away, I thought you were still awake... Nice pad, by the way. Anyway, gotta go. It was nice meeting you.'

~

Savlon, shower, shave. Off we go. It's the film wrap party for *Bridget Jones's Diary* at the In and Out, a military gentlemen's club. Wrap parties are a way of thanking everybody, cast and crew alike, who has worked on a film production and can be extremely touch and go affairs. Particularly touchy if the cast and crew, who have just endured an arduous shoot over many months, are sick of the sight of each other and would rather be inserting clapper boards up their waste holes than sharing a sherbet. Fortunately, this wrap party appears to be full of bonhomie and only serving beer and wine.

~

Off to the Isle of Wight for the millennium celebration. A clifftop party, with tons of fresh seafood and a firework display. That will do nicely. Skid's already in the year 2000 and said the Sydney harbour celebrations were beyond spectacular.

~

Although London is going to be hosting trillions of different events itself, it's actually a joy to get away from the capital for once. I don't really fancy a busman's holiday and I love the idea of starting a new century looking out to sea and fresh horizons.

~

There's talk of every computer system in the world crashing at midnight. It makes a change from streamers and Auld Lang Syne.

~

It's now 11.50 p.m. My date's copped off with someone else. At least he's only younger, richer and better looking than me. Happy New Year!

~

Soren's secured the post-Bafta Miramax party for Noble Rot on the back of Nob Rot's (as I've taken to calling it) launch party. This prestigious event is the British equivalent of the *Vanity Fair* bash that follows the Oscars and is always packed to the rafters with movie stars.

~

Miramax night. I've just been chatting with Mick Jagger about the movie *Crouching Tiger, Hidden Dragon* and comparing it to an old childhood favourite TV show of mine called *The Water Margin*. Goldie Hawn and Russell Crowe on my left, Joaquin Phoenix and Hugh Grant on my right. It's funny how, in situations like this, the major star you are talking to always assumes that you are a mate of the other major star, who you have just introduced him or her to, thereby protecting your E-list status and firmly securing your place in the inner sanctum.

~

An early morning call from Piers Hernu, a good mate who edits *Front*, a football and fanny magazine in the vein of *Loaded*.

'You around next week?'

'Why?'

'I've got a three-day freebie to Ibiza doing a piece on a company that specialises in luxury villas, yachts and clubbing tours and the missus can't make it… so, if you're up for it?'

~

Piers first came to my attention in a fly-on-the-wall documentary about the setting up of *Front* magazine. He has a brooding intensity and it came as no real surprise to me when he mentioned, not long after meeting him, that he'd spent eight months in a Nepalese jail for smuggling gold. There are definitely demons still being exorcised here and they all have altitude sickness. That said, he is funny, articulate and fine company.

~

Our evening flight from Stanstead has touched down in Ibiza at 10 p.m. when most hardcore clubbers are just getting up. Dean, our jovial host, grabs our luggage and leads us to his army jeep. Next stop Casa Azur, our Ibizan home from home for the next few days. It's a lavish abode with a gym, a bar, a swimming pool with a sliding roof, a 200-metre long roof terrace, a games room and, as an afterthought, its own nightclub.

~

A quick freshen-up and an even quicker pick-me-up and we're back in the jeep heading for Ibiza Town for some pre-club drinks. Our first stop for liquid refreshment is the Base bar, a particular favourite of the assembled 24/7ers. From the comfort of our bar stools, Piers and I drop our first Es of the night, lean back and soak up the pre-storm ambience.

~

The highly colourful procession of international hipsters, gaudy glamour queens and charged-up clubberati is becoming more vivid with every passing second.

'God, these are trippy,' I mumble to Piers, as the waiter comes to take our next drinks order. 'I'm glad I only took two.'

~

By the time we hit the Ministry of Sound's night at Pacha (the self-billed king of Ibizan clubs), I've left Earth's atmosphere. We slide past security, who all give Dean a friendly punch, and head for the main dance floor. The crowd are already close to fever pitch. I'm wandering around in circles in a beatific daze. I've became totally disorientated with the layout of the club. A concerned-looking couple want to know if I'm ok.

'Yes, I'm really great, thanks.'

'Yeah, we know you are really great, but are you ok?'

~

I must look like a lost kid outside the school gates whose parents have failed to turn up. I certainly feel like it. Piers has just materialised from nowhere and informed me that we're leaving. We've been in Pacha for four hours. It feels like 20 minutes.

~

Dean's woken me up with a strong coffee. It's 7 p.m. People are starting to arrive for tonight's party at the villa. Danny Rampling's spinning for 200 or so people, so it should be a night to remember... or not. Just wish I didn't feel so rough. Luckily, someone's firing up the barbecue. I haven't eaten a thing since leaving London. Fuck, I'm starving.

~

A plate of chicken wings and a mountain of new potatoes have definitely put the colour back in my cheeks. Time to rehydrate with a couple of cold beers. I'm chatting with a cute, in a hippy kind of way, local girl. She's just popped a couple of pills in my mouth. Here we go again.

~

'Fuck, you missed a blinding party.'

I've just come to.

'Dean and I had to carry you to bed. Can't believe that bird mixed up the Es with the Zeeeees.'

~

Our last night. A quick stomach liner as the sun sets at the Mambo bar in San Antonio, the white island's second town, which plays Mr Hyde to Ibiza Town's Dr Jeckyll, then off to KM5 for a few shots and finally to Space. This part-al fresco club is right under the flight path and enables you to wave at the overhead jet that should be returning you home. I'm on the drug wagon tonight as we have a 4 a.m. flight to catch and without the aid of stimulants the last five hours have felt like... well, five hours.

~

We've just landed at Luton. I feel like I'm about to give birth. I have an excruciating pain in my stomach. Charing Cross Hospital here I come.

~

The scan has determined that my left kidney has stopped draining and the ensuing build-up of fluid is causing the terrible pain.

'Oh, and it looks like you've got pancreatitis.'

~

The tests are back from my doctor. They confirm that I do indeed have pancreatitis. He has suggested a total abstinence from alcohol and drugs.

~

Oh the irony in my 'glass full to the brim' philosophy.

~

I've started smoking for the first time. I'm 39.

~

I'm at the launch of a high street clothing label in an old embassy building in Belgravia. They've decked out the main room as a mini casino with roulette and blackjack tables. We've all been given ten chips. The person with the most at the end of the evening will win a trip for two to Las Vegas.

~

I'm on a roll. Eight straight wins and a mountain of chips. Just having them counted. Vegas here I come.

~

'And in second place… Nick Valentine.'

~

I've been cheated. I clearly saw that the jubilant winner had half as many chips as me, but unfortunately (for me) she works for *Vogue*. Second prize is a supermarket sweep in Essex.

~

My taxi driver is very excited about my prize that I've just donated to him and will not accept payment for my fare.

~

A tearful phone call from Colin. His wife has left him.

~

Life as a teetotaller certainly has its advantages. I'm sleeping better, looking better and have discovered the simple pleasure of afternoon tea. Today it's Claridge's. Lovely spread. What a difference a day makes. The last time I was here I was partying in a suite with a famous personal trainer friend of mine and a group of female gym junkies he had picked up at the Hippodrome earlier that evening, one of whom unfortunately decided to redecorate the lounge area with the fetid contents of her stomach. To this day, the smell of a protein shake makes me gag.

~

It's strange being at parties sober. I'm now acutely aware of all the drunken behaviour around me. I was thinking last night how dull everyone was, then the truth slowly dawned … it's actually me who's the crushing bore.

~

Sobriety takes a great deal of adjustment. The urge to carry on partying after a press event, dinner or whatever is considerably less when you've spent the night on Evian. An obvious advantage is I'm no longer waking up in a different flat/town/county/country/ outfit after yet another bender.

~

I have to vacate the flat in Putney as my mate's back from Brazil and wants his gaff back. I've found a nice house-share in Chiswick. My new bedroom opens out directly on to the garden, which I've started tending to with childlike enthusiasm every time the snow melts. I've started waking up around 6 a.m., normally the time I got to bed when I was drinking.

~

I've enrolled for tango lessons. I'm the only guy in the class. Slowly picking up all the moves… the female moves.

~

Off to Mexico. Colin is treating me to a two-week, all-inclusive holiday to get over his break-up. I'm in Boots at Heathrow Airport stocking up on holiday essentials; three boxes of Imodium and some extra-strong mints. Here comes Colin. I hardly recognise him in his new wrap-around shades, lime green nylon shirt, high-waisted flared jeans and Great Gatsby shoes. He looks like he got dressed in the dark, high on mescaline.

'What the *fuck* are you wearing?'

'I'm single now, mate. Gotta get noticed.'

~

Colin always turns pulling into panto. Strange voices spout forth from his mouth and complete new characters emerge from beneath his Mr Newton hat. By the time he should be going in for the kill, he's normally put on such a dramatic performance that he's actually more interested in his own company and returns home alone, content and thoroughly entertained.

~

Another quirk of Colin's is that he is always joking with me about how competitive we were with each other over women in our teens. I remind him that I wasn't competitive at all. I would start dating a girl and then he'd try and pinch her off me. He recalls it the other way around, of course. One floozy who dated both of us once exclaimed that one of us was better in bed and the other more interesting. We stayed up quite late that night trying to decide which one we would rather be and were still quite unsure by the time we hit the Horlicks.

~

The all-inclusive resort in Cancun reminds me of my first family holiday to Butlins in 1970 without the elation of coming second in the Happy Smile competition. Colin and I have decided to cut our losses and head south.

~

In Playa del Carmen we've found what we'd been hoping for: beach bars with rustic charm, low-rise dwellings, family-run restaurants, indigenous shops and backpacking beauties, all on a mile-long strip of sea-washed and sun-dried, travel-brochure white sand.

~

I'm chilling on our terrace listening to Coldplay on Colin's latest gadget: the iPod. I need to get one. It's an OCD sufferer's dream come true. I can't buy a CD, no matter how much I like the contents, if the name of the artist is the wrong way up on the spine or if the disc itself has an image on it.

~

We're checking out the local tavern. Moonshine shots and paracetamol chasers for Colin, served by a bird with a beard. The Good, the bad and the ugly. Freshly squeezed orange juice for me, with lots of ice.

'Same again, please.'

~

Imodium.

~

'I told you last night not to have ice.'

~

More Imodium.

~

A cork.

~

Voluntary euthanasia.

~

Not really the best end to a holiday. I'm looking pretty trim though.

~

I've invented a board game called Icon based on the old Rizla-on-the-forehead party piece. Basically, the player puts on a celebrity mask without knowing who it is and, through a serious of carded questions, has to work out whose identity they have assumed. I've managed to sell shares in the idea for £12,000, so I'm off to Jermyn Street for some retail therapy.

~

Eight new shirts. If I see something I like, I buy it in every colour, though my OCD only allows me to buy equal numbers, so I can never just buy one of anything. Suits are the exception, for no discernible reason.

~

My flatmates have obviously noticed I'm a neat freak. They constantly move things around in my room just to see if I notice… I always do.

~

I'm working on another adult parlour game called Swinger. 'Throw A Double, You're In Trouble'. You get the picture.

~

I spoke to Skid at length last night. He is trying to formulate a plan to move back to England in a year or so, now that his kids are old enough to live between Australia and the UK. It would be great to have him here again. He's been away for 19 years.

~

The fizz has definitely gone out of my party lifestyle and not just the bubbles that I'm no longer drinking. I need a new direction and a change of scene. I just don't know what.

~

I know what. I hooked up with a cute American medical student called Alicia a few nights ago at an American Independence Day dinner. She's moving back to the States next week, so I've just jacked in the job at *Entertainment News* and told her I'm coming too.

~

Farewell drinks with Colin. He thinks I'm nuts. I know it's a bit of a reckless move, shooting off to live in a new country with someone I barely know, but it's made me feel alive again.

~

A silver stretch limo waiting for us at JFK airport. This is the life.

First stop Cooperstown in upstate New York to meet the parents.

~

I feel like I'm in an episode of *The Waltons*. Home for the next few weeks is a beautiful wooden farmhouse, with the obligatory rocking chair on the porch. Ma and Pa are very cool and seem very unfazed by my impulsive act.

~

Alicia will resume her studies in Virginia in September, so we've decided to take a road trip in the interim. First stop, a trek across the border into Canada.

~

We've been driving for a few hours across cinematic landscapes, with only the roadkill we further flatten every few miles for company. There seems to be a proliferation of dead snakes on the highway, so when I get Alicia to pull up at the side of the road so I can take a leak, I need an immense amount of assurance that it will be safe. As I zip up my fly and stroll back to the car a huge, slobbering bear pops out from behind the tree I've just relieved myself on. I'm back in the passenger seat faster than the speed of the sound of a grown man screaming.

'Fuck me, that was close. Why didn't you mention any bears?'

''Cos you only asked about the snakes.'

~

We've just cruised flat out through five states to get to Lexington, Virginia. It's a very quaint town and my new home for the foreseeable future. I have just about enough savings to last for six months or so without working, though need to find something to occupy my time as Alicia is going to be full on at university.

~

I've bought a battered old guitar from our neighbour and spent the day trying to write a country tune. When in Rome.

~

The track's sounding great, though I've depressed the fuck out of myself. I'm eight bars away from a hit and seven bars away from suicide watch.

~

I dropped by Alicia's university earlier to watch my first game of American football. I got some very weird looks when I started photographing the cheerleaders.
    'Don't worry, he's a Brit, not a nonce.'

~

I'm watching the morning news. They are playing horrific footage of a plane hitting one of the twin towers of the World Trade Centre. As I call out to Alicia to come and watch the report, a second plane unbelievably ploughs into the other tower.

~

Alicia and I are still in a stunned silence from yesterday's events. It feels like nothing is ever going to be the same again. It's impossible to comprehend the sheer scale of what has just happened.

~

It really is a fucked up world right now and I guess things are about to get a whole lot worse.

~

I'm back in New York for a few days to meet up with Colin who's over for the weekend. It's been a good few months since 9/11 but the city is still in shock. We've checked in to The Paramount, Ian Shrager's Philippe Starck-designed, ferociously fashionable hotel on West 46th street and headed out to take in the sights.

~

Over to East 47th Street where the ghost of Andy Warhol's Factory resides. I'm hoping to feel the presence of the man who showed the world the art of repetition and then showed it again.

~

As Colin and I make our way across Central Park, 840 acres of former swampland, 'New York, New York' pops in to my head. I can clearly remember my father Tom belting out Sinatra's classic in a Palma old town dive: an open mic warm-up slot before the live sex show, the magician and the flamenco dance troupe. Those wild times in Majorca seem like a lifetime ago now.

~

Alicia's finished university so we've moved to Annapolis, Maryland. It's a cool little town and I'm very fond of her, but my life's starting to feel like *Groundhog Day*. I'm someone who needs a project to get their teeth into or I start crawling up the wall and the OCD kicks in, in a big way. I'm not quite at the stage of not being able to tread on the cracks in the pavement, but I'm getting pretty close. Time to head home.

~

Now, did I turn the oven, kitchen tap and bedroom lights off?

~

A tearful goodbye at the airport. We've promised to stay in touch. I've been away for eight months, but it feels like eight years as I touch down at Heathrow Airport.

~

I'm back on Colin's couch until I get myself sorted. It's great to have a nice strong cup of tea and indulge in a bit of British banter. The American sense of humour is very literal.

'So, I don't get it. Why did he have pineapple rings on his cock in the first place?'

~

Entertainment News has welcomed me back. It's like I never left. I bumped into a friend at a launch party last night and they commented that they hadn't seen me out on the town last week.

~

Jamie Bloom, my old t'ai chi teacher, has offered to rent me a room in his three-storey Mayfair flat, with a lovely communal garden, just off Park Lane. It's good to be back in the thick of it.

~

Jamie has a long history in the fashion and entertainment industry, having in his time owned parts of Camden Market, Crazy Larry's, The O Bar, Madame JoJo's and The Rainbow Theatre, among others. While The Rainbow was under his tenure, it played host to all manner of rock 'n' roll and country legends, including The Who, Lynyrd Skynyrd, Chuck Berry, Iggy Pop, The Ramones and Dolly Parton, who apparently was the only ever act to use the on-site showers, installed at great expense.

~

The Clash also famously performed at The Rainbow one night, sparking a full-scale riot that resulted in 600 seats being trashed, though Jamie miraculously managed to replace them in time for the following evening's show, by the rather less rebellious Slade.

~

A weekend away at Jamie Bloom's villa in Marbella. It's 90 degrees in the shade. The local estate agent has dropped by to value the property and caught us playing ping pong in our undies. He keeps referring to me as Jamie's partner.

~

We've taken a table at the Olivia Valere nightclub, a local establishment dressed up like a Hollywood biblical epic. All that's missing is scantily clad nymphets proffering grapes... I tell a lie.

~

My 40th birthday at the Cobden Club in Kensal Road. Founder members had to supply a book for the library. I donated Bertrand Russell's *Why I Am Not a Christian*. Someone nicked it on the first night. The receptionist said they won't go to heaven.

'Because they now know it doesn't exist.'

~

Colin's got lucky with an E... Emma. Ditto E... E. I love the DJ etc., etc.

~

I've misplaced all my presents from last night, somewhere between Shepherd's and hairy.

~

Entertainment News has moved to new offices in Covent Garden. As I am only there a few days a week I have to share a desk. Consequently, the first hour of my working day generally involves half a kitchen roll, some pungent cleaning fluid and a lot of rearranging.

~

Skid has moved back to England. It's great to have him here again. He's taken a job as a chauffeur, so I'm being driven around in fine style on his nights off. His new career was nearly dramatically cut short when his first-ever customer, upon being told that he could not smoke in the back, tried to chuck his fag out of the window and lobbed it down the back of Skid's shirt instead. As my brother endeavoured to put out the butt with his back, he nearly caused a major pile-up on the Chiswick roundabout.

'And the bell-end was more concerned that it was his last smoke.'

~

Dinner with Skid at the Harrington Club, Ronnie Wood's members' club in South Kensington, then drinks around the corner at Boujis, a new boutique, i.e. tiny, club. It reminds me of the clubs along the Cala Mayor strip in Majorca that my father and I used to go to in the mid-80s. I remember one particular supposed hotspot where it took 30 minutes of serious blagging to get past the door into, much to our surprise, a totally empty club.

~

Skid cannot believe how much London has changed. When he left the UK in the early 80s, it was still the era of flock wallpaper, illegal lock-ins and warm beer served in a Watney's glass, and that was just in our family living room.

~

I've teamed up with Julian Stewart Lindsay again under the moniker Super Paradise and started working on a chill-out concept album called *From the Beach to the Bedroom*. I've just road-tested a couple of the tracks in my boudoir and it seems the performance coming from my stereo is more highly rated than that on the king-size and only one of the two is getting a request for an encore.

'Nice accordion riff.'

~

Another outing from Mourad Mazouz. Sketch is a grandiose new space in Conduit Street with a couple of bars and restaurants and giant egg-shaped loos. It must have cost a king's ransom to complete. They still have a few teething troubles though, one being the locks on the hatching crappers that kept me prisoner for about 20 minutes last night.

~

I've picked up my new glasses. IC Berlin. Unbreakable. I'm thinking *Easy Rider*!
    'Easy listening,' corrects Colin.

~

A family Christmas at my sister Jane's new house in Inverness. She is back in fine health and on great form. It's the first time us siblings have been all in the same room together since my father died. I take the chance to rummage through some old family photo albums from the early 70s. It's like looking at stills from Mike Leigh's comedy of manners, *Abigail's Party*. In one standing snap, my shirt collar is literally touching our yellow and green swirl shagpile, and that's in four-inch platform boots.

~

To the Alexander McQueen store launch party. I've met him a few times before when I was dating a girl called Danny who studied fashion at Central St Martins College. She was in the same year as Stella McCartney and was seriously upstaged at her graduation ceremony when Kate Moss and Yasmin Le Bon strutted down the catwalk in Stella's creations. I was more fucked off than Danny, having spent half the night helping her put the final stitches to her collection, a nimble skill picked up from my mother.

~

Early drinks for the launch of PR supremo Liz Brewer's book, *The Party Bible*. Not long after meeting Liz, she kindly introduced me to her good friend Shirley Bassey at a charity ball one night. Shirley was my mother's all-time favourite singer. I mentioned this to Shirley and she rather dramatically started to sing one of her many classics a cappella to me. What I failed to mention was that when my father left my mother for a short while, after he'd had a brief disastrous affair with one of my mother's best friends, Shirley's 'Days of Wine and Roses' became the soundtrack and morbid backdrop to my mother's ensuing melancholia and mine by association. As Shirley regally moved on, my bottom lip started doing the rumba and I inadvertently invented the teardrop Martini.

~

I've started doing some consultancy work on the side for a company called Bleach PR, owned by an old friend Inge Theron. It specialises in luxury goods. She's asked me if I fancy helping organise a boat party they are hosting for a diamond client during the Cannes Film Festival. The answer is obviously yes and as I pick up my cream linen suit from the dry cleaners, I'm feeling pretty chuffed for a boy from the sticks who left school with four O-levels, and one of them being Religious Education, so that doesn't count.

~

Inge and I have stopped by for a drink at the bar of the Hotel du Cap-Eden-Roc to discuss tomorrow night's event. If Madame Tussaud's owned a bar, this is what it would look like. Cameron Diaz on my left, Uma Thurman on my right and Jack Black's just joined our table. We seem to be the only people here that aren't Hollywood royalty, though my English accent carries me through until closing time.

~

The boat party is going well, though this floating palace seems to be getting rather trashed. Boy band Blue are among the guests of honour. I'm still not drinking alcohol so it's an early night for me.

~

We sailed through the night and have docked in Monaco. Unfortunately, I left the only pair of shoes I brought with me on the jetty in Cannes and we have a black tie dinner tonight. I will try and buy a new pair in Monaco, though it's extremely difficult to get footwear when you are a size 12.

~

Flip-flops and tuxedo. Not a good look.

~

A week's recharge in London and I'm back with Inge in Monaco. This time for 'Flawless Engineering', a five-day extravaganza around the Monaco Grand Prix in association with The Diamond Trading Company, Steinmetz, Moussaieff and the Jaguar Racing Team. The highlight of the event, which includes a VIP gala dinner, a press conference and a fashion shoot featuring Danish supermodel Helena Christensen, is the unveiling of the 59.6-carat flawless Steinmetz pink diamond – the Monaco Rose. My job is to chaperone Helena to the various photocalls and perform all manner of minor chores for a fashion shoot with Naomi Campbell, an arduous task as Naomi is not known for her punctuality and time is very tight.

~

Helena is lovely and very easy-going. Naomi is Naomi.

~

At a photo shoot with Jaguar's lead driver, Marc Webber. The iconic white Jaguar leaper logo has been replaced with a pink one for the race, in honour of the Monaco Rose, I'm told.

~

It's rather strange being in such close proximity to Marc, a master of his craft, yet having practically next to no interest in his sport. In fact, I must be the only non-petrolhead in a good ten-mile radius.

~

Dinner with Hollywood A-lister Wesley Snipes. He is a guest of one of the sponsors and is being photographed next to the track tomorrow. He is 'Just call me Wes' chilled, philosophical and amusing. A pleasant surprise.

~

Strolling with Wes to the photo shoot. He has no entourage/ minders and suggests we stop off at a café. We are immediately mobbed by fans, but he takes it all in his (slow) stride.

~

I'm in a prime place, courtesy of Jaguar, watching my first Grand Prix. It's actually, dare I admit it, extremely exciting, which is a shock, but also totally deafening. It's sign language all the way. Someone's just signed to me to say Marc Webber has pulled out as his engine has lost air pressure… or were they just having a good scratch?

~

Out with Wes for the night. We are off to the first-ever Amber Lounge, a pop-up, post-Grand Prix club started by Formula 1 driver Eddie Irvine's sister, Sonia. Black suit, black shirt, black tie. I'm mourning my pancreas. I started drinking again last night.

~

We've run into Bono and The Edge at the entrance and have all been ushered to the star chamber. I'm hovering. Looking sharp. Bono's motioning me over. He wants a word. Cool... very cool.

'Can we get some more ice, please?'

~

It's a week on and I'm still deaf from the Grand Prix. Colin keeps asking me why I'm shouting at him... I think that's what he said.

~

Another consultancy job for Touch Media, a new boutique agency specialising in fashion and beauty PR. They want to get out and about and believe I'm the man to open doors for them, so to speak. Not literally, I hope.

~

It's the morning after my first night of 'door opening' and three of the girls at Touch Media haven't made it into the office today. They've suggested I cut our evenings out down to once a week, or at least until they are all back on solids.

~

Terribly sad news from Skid. His son Lucas has committed suicide. He is devastated and completely baffled.

~

Skid's returned to Australia for the funeral. No words can console a parent who loses their child in this manner.

~

I'm still in a state of total shock. It seems like only yesterday that Lucas was tottering towards the Sydney Gay and Lesbian Mardi Gras in six-inch stilettos, towering above his fellow revellers, larger than life itself.

~

A very solemn coffee with Skid. He has already lost a stone in weight and is in a right old state. I feel so dreadfully sorry for him and Domini and Lucas's siblings.

~

It feels weird being out on the lash while my brother descends into such a painfully rapid meltdown. I don't quite know what to say or do.

~

A melancholically appropriate night out to see ex-Rolling Stone Mick Taylor's blues band. A musical genre born of loss and tragedy.

~

Skid is struggling with every second of every day. He's told me it's as if he's gone into remote control mode. Get up, don't eat, go to bed. Get up…

~

Another event for Bleach PR. This time in Lebanon for Mouawad, a multinational jewellery and watch design company founded in 1890. (They have just created the most expensive piece of lingerie ever made for Victoria's Secret and modelled by Heidi Klum, called The Very Sexy Fantasy Bra. $11,000,000, to be precise.) I am to accompany former Steps singer Lisa Scott Lee to a gala evening at the luxurious Grand Hills Hotel and Spa, where she will perform her first solo single, 'Too Far Gone'.

~

I've settled into my appointed suite and now joined Lisa and her fiancé Johnny Shentall for breakfast. The television news in the lobby has just worryingly flashed a report of a bomb blast in the city.
'More tea?'

~

An evening at Crystal nightclub. A teaser of Beirut nightlife before tomorrow's extravaganza. I've lost count of the quickly quaffed cocktails consumed. A final Tom Collins and it's time to head back to the hotel, past the strange juxtaposition of glisteningly new skyscrapers and the shells of bombed-out, war-torn buildings.

~

'Thank you, thank you.'
Much applause for Lisa. She and Johnny are off to bed. I'm off to party. Contrary to what I've been told, the Lebanese are very hospitable people and have to be highly commended for their stoical approach to life in such a deeply troubled region… and the grub's pretty good, too.

~

At Speedo's 75th birthday celebration. I'm a big fan of the look of their 1950s-style trunks, though, no matter how much repositioning I do I always end up with one ball making a break for sunlight. I'm sure Sean Connery never had that problem.

~

My fashion sense has always been fairly retro. The 70s is an era I'm particularly drawn to. Flared trousers are very flattering when you have big feet and skinny ankles and brown and orange are colours that prompt very happy childhood memories for me, though I draw the line at avocado.

~

I've never been a fan of designer labels. In fact, I cut the label out of any new clothing purchase. This can prove to be incredibly annoying when, as I've done from time to time, I cut straight through the label and into the garment, necessitating that I go straight back to the shop and buy an exact replacement.

~

To the ICA to see the masters of melodrama Suede play to a sold-out house. Their style and sound is very reminiscent of my old band Mardou, so I guess we were ahead of our time, or just another group of young guys with a healthy Bowie obsession.

~

A press screening of yet another insipid rom-com. That's a select group of journos given an advance chance to rate or slate the latest reels of moving images in convivial, intimate surroundings. To me this is the only way to see a movie, apart from in the comfort of your own home. I'm not a fan of the public auditorium, cinema experience. For some bizarre reason, the second I'm sat with more than about 20 people for any kind of mass showing I start coughing. It's involuntary and perverse because I know it's the one thing I shouldn't do. A bit like getting a hard-on in a public pool.

~

I've just been chastised. No, not for coughing, there were only 19 people in the screening room... no, snoring. I don't know what all the fuss is about. I see it as an honest review.

~

Jamie's doing some extensive building work at his house, so I've moved into the Pont Street Hotel in Knightsbridge which he co-owns, for six weeks. I've had a micro-clear-out and paired down

my possessions to a bare minimum, which is just as well as the
wardrobe space is, to put it kindly, rather nominal. My father Tom
did the same when he sailed off into the sunset after my mother's
death. It's given me a magnificent sense of freedom, though I am
rather deliberating about my 1962 Fender Precision bass.

~

I've decided to keep my bass. I ran into my old mate Dale Davis,
who played on all of my Baseland tracks, this morning and when
he offered to buy it off me I knew I couldn't sell it. It's strange
how you can get emotionally attached to an inanimate object. It's
probably how my love interest in *Brothers* felt.

~

Dale's just started working with a new singer called Amy Winehouse
and has invited me to a recording they're doing for *Later... with
Jools Holland*. Now, taking into account his considerable talent, he's
probably the most un-up-himself guy I have ever met.

~

A telephone call from Nick Rhodes. He has asked me to organise an
after-party for Duran Duran. They are to receive the Outstanding
Contribution to Music Award at the Brit Awards in February and
want to continue partying after the show in Earls Court. Nick also
lived in a hotel for a while, albeit the slightly more salubrious Savoy.

~

It's the Cross nightclub's 10th anniversary party tonight. Ten years
is a massive achievement for any venue in London, with most
undercutting the lifespan of a sick butterfly.

~

I'm back living in Mayfair. I'm sure going to miss room service and the joy of going out without a house key.

~

My friend Azzy Asghar publishes a luxury lifestyle magazine called *Epicurean Life* and has asked me to write a travel piece for him, so I'm off to Hong Kong and China with my new squeeze Meili Li, who I met in the Pont Street Hotel spa.

~

Hong Kong's just finding its feet again after the recent SARS crisis torpedoed its tourist industry and visitor numbers are down but it's still one of the most densely populated areas on the globe. If everyone on Hong Kong Island flushes their loo simultaneously, you can probably walk Moses-like to Kowloon. It's the high-rise living and breathing embodiment of East meets West, where colourful ancient traditions and colonial hand-downs sit comfortably side by side and I love it.

~

We've checked into the Island Shangri-La Hotel and ascended to the Deluxe Harbour room on the 54th floor, with a view straight out of *Bladerunner*. I'm all up for a kip, but my Chinese companion is insisting on dragging me to Hong Kong Park's fish ponds, where she hopes to tune up her Taoism, one of the three main religions practised here, Buddhism and Confucianism being the other two.

~

I'm all Tao'd out and happy to get the tram up to Victoria Park, where the price per square foot of the surrounding area's real estate makes Belgravia look 'up and coming'.

~

A final bit of retail therapy before we hit mainland China. Meili has a third dan in shopping and places it two places above sex and one above chocolate. I'm a bit peckish, so have stopped at one of the many street vendors and bought a couple of satay sticks called dragon's kiss.

~

It's been four hours since my roadside snack and I still can't feel my tongue. I swear I stopped breathing for a few minutes at some stage, but Mrs 'It's A Little Bit Spicy' reckons I'm making a fuss over nothing. I've just smoked three fags without the need for a lighter and I'm hoping the hotel's concierge service can book me in for a general anaesthetic before my next trip to the khazi.

~

A bit of spiritual nourishment at the Guang-xiao Temple, having passed on the lunchtime offering of snake, snake or snake at 'one of China's finest eateries'. I've been offered a 'genuine Rolex', 'redemption' and a chance to converse with any dead relatives and I've only been here ten minutes.

~

Tom's fine, by the way.

~

Duran Duran seem to be enjoying themselves. Adam Street members' club is just starting to fill up with a mix of Duran family members, music industry bods and celebrity fans. Nick's just introduced me to Scarlett Johansson, though I thought he said it was his niece and so embarrassingly told her she was a dead ringer for...

~

Justin Timberlake, who earlier this evening won the Brits' Best

International Male Solo Artist, is holding court at one end of the room, Stephen Fry and Gwen Stefani the other, while female DJ duo Queens of Noize are keeping everybody entertained with what seems like the soundtrack to my life so far.

~

I've dragged Skid out to the *Kath and Kim* DVD launch party, with Kath and Kim in attendance. I love the series. Mother and daughter are pretty much the same age in real life. Skid switches to a really strong Aussie accent within seconds of meeting them. I tend to do the cockney equivalent with taxi drivers after a couple of pints for no real reason, while expressing a sudden out-of-character interest in politics.

~

It's *Loaded* magazine's tenth birthday party. I cannot believe it's been ten years. I'm obviously ageing on the outside, but feel no different within. I'm 41 going on 14 and, sadly, still care who is Number 1 in the charts and how low my Levi's hang. My sister puts it down to me never having had children.

~

A weekend away at Julian Dunkerton's house in Cheltenham. I haven't seen him since our week in Zakynthos last summer, where I cracked two teeth biting into an olive stone, then broke three toes and a couple of ribs when the brakes on my moped failed and I had to make a split-second decision and jump off the bike before it hit the car in front.

~

Julian has rebranded his Cult Clothing company. It's now called Superdry.

~

I have been invited to the La Dolce Vita Ball at the 18th-century Stowe House in Buckingham before the British Grand Prix at Silverstone. My proposed date says she has nothing to wear, so I've called in a favour from my old friend Alice Temperley, who was actually an extra in *Brothers* before becoming one of the top fashion designers in the industry.

~

Gordon Ramsay has cooked dinner and Beyoncé is performing live in the grounds later, so my date is obviously very pleased to be here. She looks amazing in Alice's floor-length sequinned dress. So amazing, in fact, that she's caught the attention of quite a few admirers. One of them has just kindly offered to show her where the ladies' loo is located.

~

It's been an hour or more and still no sign of my date. I guess her admirer's sense of direction wasn't that good.

~

A beach party at The Great Eastern, a former Victorian railway hotel next to Liverpool Street Station. They've shipped in a ton of sand and Punch and Judy'ed it to the shoreline. I'm stripped to the waist and there's room for two in my surfer shorts, so I'm on the hunt. Unfortunately, my creator got a bit muddled and gave me my father's enthusiasm and my mother's muscles.

~

I was out till daybreak at the launch of The British Luxury Club. There seems to be a new club opening every other week at the moment and at least as many closing.

~

Off to the première of Paul Bettany's new film, *Wimbledon*. Now Paul's a remarkable actor, but I imagine this has even surpassed the *Brothers* trailer as one on-screen outing that he would rather forget.

~

A quick drink with ex-Stranglers frontman Hugh Cornwell at the launch of his debut novel. Hugh was another act I got to play at the annual Inns of Court Ball. It was rather surreal that night, watching the cream of the UK's legal profession bopping along to 'Golden Brown', an ode to the joys of heroin use.

~

I'm as happy as Lorenzo at the launch of Floridita, a new Cuban-themed restaurant/bar in Soho. The Buena Vista Social Club are performing tonight. They are both totally brilliant and extremely ancient. I'm wondering if they will live long enough to play an encore.

~

Another club launch. This time The Penthouse. Skid keeps suggesting that I should somehow open my own place.

~

Off to Thailand for Christmas and New Year for some R&R.

~

I'm canoeing on the crystal-clear Andaman Sea off Railay West beach in Krabi. It's still a relatively unspoilt paradise with a comatose vibe. I can't think of anywhere else I would rather be spending Christmas Day. Eddie (an old mate from London who now lives in Thailand) and I are making the most of the wonderful weather. Tonight we have to take the 30-minute longboat trip around the peninsula to Ao Nang, so that we can spend one night near the car hire place, a couple of hundred metres from the seafront, and make an early start on our journey up to Bangkok.

~

My bed is moving across the floor towards Eddie's.
    'Fuck, mate, I think we're having an earthquake.'
    'No… that's the hangover kicking in. We better get moving, though.'

~

We've driven a couple of miles inland and stopped for petrol. The flickering television on the forecourt is transmitting horrific news. We have just driven away, Mr Magoo-like, from the most devastating tsunami in mankind's history, with waves as high as 98 feet recorded and the magnitude of the earthquake measured as 9.1 on the Richter scale.

~

I'm watching Sky News at Eddie's flat in Bangkok. The scale of the disaster is almost too much to comprehend. It's frightening to think I was paddling around in a pond-calm bay only hours before the tsunami struck.

~

The whole country is mourning the inconsolable loss of mothers and fathers, brothers and sisters, husbands and wives. My friend James called me earlier from Phuket and told me that some tourists are still, unbelievably, sunbathing on the beaches there while dead bodies intermittently wash up on the shore.

~

Back in England. I'm still touched by the taxi driver who drove me to Bangkok airport and would not accept my fare against prolonged protestation, only asking me that I make a promise to return to his country. He is, no doubt, already painfully aware of the economic catastrophe that is sure to follow the colossal human tragedy, in a country so reliant on tourism.

~

The total loss of life is now estimated at 230,000 people across 14 countries.

~

Skid and I have been batting a few clichés about life and death back and forwards to each other. In truth, we've both seen death up closer than we would otherwise choose to and certainly share a *carpe diem* mentality, based on our individual and collective losses.

~

An early evening drink with Jamie Lorenz and his father Bobby. They have asked me to help set up a new members' club and just need to find a venue for sale in a good location.

~

Emma Sayle, a fairly new acquaintance, wants to know if I would like to work with her on the PR for Erotica UK, an adult consumer exhibition that describes itself as 'The world's largest lifestyle show for freethinking adults who are comfortable with their sexuality.'
    'Yes please.'

~

The PR has gone fairly well, but today's Erotica exhibition at the G-Mex Manchester seems to be lacking serious footfall. I'm hoping tonight's event will be busier.

~

The fetish club Torture Garden is hosting the exhibition after-party, so it's a quick pit stop back at the hotel, a shower and a light snack before I squeeze into tonight's specially purchased outfit.

~

I'm a rubber virgin and have nearly dislocated both arms trying to get my midnight black one-piece jumpsuit on. Emma says I just need a lot more talc, though I'm starting to seriously resemble Frosty the Snowman, particularly with the new platinum white cropped locks.

~

I've been at the party for ten minutes. Someone's just asked me if I've come as a pint of Guinness.

~

Emma's introduced me to a rather seductive burlesque performer called Kitty Klaw. I'm chewing the fat with her and the Honourable Henry Fromanteel Lytton-Cobbold, who is also working with Erotica UK. Henry trained as a screenwriter, but is best perhaps known as being a rather unconventional lord of the manor, his manor being the gothic Knebworth House, the legendary stately home and sometime rock venue. He has invited me down for afternoon tea next week and has surprised me with the admission that he has never tried an alcoholic drink in his life.

'And you?'

~

The good news is I've pulled a Betty Page lookalike. The bad news is I'm back at her hotel and can't get my outfit off.

~

I'm nosing around Knebworth House. It's been Henry's family seat since 1490. One of Henry's ancestors was the Victorian author and statesman Edward Bulwer-Lytton, who coined the phrase 'The pen is mightier than the sword.' Try telling that to Anne Boleyn.

~

Henry says that when the Rolling Stones played here in 1976, he was 14 years old and far more interested in that evening's episode of *Star Trek* than watching the world's greatest rock 'n' roll band perform. Consequently, he was rather hacked off when a somewhat determined guy interrupted his favourite television show by repeatedly banging on the back door, so as to be let into the concert after-party. Paul McCartney's obviously not a fan of *Star Trek*.

~

A rather jovial guy I met at Erotica is helping organise a massive VIP swingers' party called Fever, at a five-storey townhouse just off Oxford Street on Saturday. Fever's membership list is an ultra-exclusive mix of models, politicians, bankers, lawyers, actresses, captains of industry and the founders' close friends, who all regularly meet up for a touch of ribaldry at various luxurious and discreet locations in and around London. Mr Jolly needs three DJs – one to play house music, one to play funk and soul and another for the chill-out area – and has asked me if I know anyone who fits the bill. I've cheerily offered my spinning services for the chill-out slot and recommended a couple of friends for the house and funkier slots.

~

Much to my fellow DJs' annoyance, I've been given the orgy room while my two compadres have been shown to the dance floor and reception area, respectively. Couples and single girls are slowly starting to trickle in. Nine double beds have been pushed together to create a giant, satin-clad bonking arena. It's certainly given me a focal point. I've decided to kick off proceedings and create the right mood with Albinoni's Adagio in G minor. It's all terribly civilised. A touch too civilised, perhaps, as a slim, busty brunette in her early 20s and her partner, a shaven-headed guy of indeterminable age with a bodybuilder's physique, have rather interrupted the seductive tempo I'm trying to set with a fine display of fellatio, thereby declaring the sexual Olympics officially open.

~

Within minutes of the first starting pistol going off, everyone is at it. The assembled players have formed a heaving carnal scrum on the 25-yard line and both sides appear to be pressing for the conversion. Couples, trios, foursomes, fivesomes... are going head to toe, toe to toe, head to head and a few other imaginative competitive manoeuvres I don't think I've ever encountered before. Hats off to the guy who's just performed an impressive triple jump. Some participants are going for the sprint, others the long distance, but everyone's pushing for gold with a select few exceptions who are happy to settle for brass.

~

It's been a couple of hours or so and it's now very difficult to differentiate whose arm, leg, head or cock belongs to which writhing participant. The master volume on my decks is pushing 11 and yet the orgasmic grunting is still drowning out my lilting Arabic beats. Mr House and Mr Funk have deserted their posts and joined my side, curious to see this unbelievably torrid spectacle exploding before them.

~

Three hours in and quite frankly it's a bit of a turn-off. The initial cheap thrill of nudity and naughtiness has been replaced with, dare I say it, a slight yawning boredom. It's just all too mechanical, too unemotional. More groping gladiators than romping Raphaelites. I've even started caring about what music I play. Would Frank Sinatra's *Songs for Swinging Lovers* be too obvious? Mind you, most of the assembled guests are either sunk to the nuts or so otherwise engrossed I think I could play the best of Megadeth and no one would give a shit.

~

Skid reckons that was the only event in history where the DJs were the only people who *didn't* get laid.

~

The party has made the front page of the *Sunday Mirror*. Some salacious sneak evidently smuggled a camera into the house and captured all of the swinging shenanigans on film.

~

My phone hasn't stopped ringing all day with people asking me when the next Fever party is.

~

To the launch of Julian Clary's biography *A Young Man's Passage* at Soho House with Skid. Julian and I were born in the same police flats in Surbiton and our mothers were best friends for years, but I haven't seen him in donkey's. He is actually quite shy in real life, as a lot of outré comedians tend to be. I remind him of an aborted spring afternoon we spent in childhood, trying to mate our respective Abyssinian guinea pigs. They both turned out to be sows.

~

Jamie Lorenz has found a Danish investor called Bo Bendtsen and a vacant site in Swallow Street in Mayfair for the proposed new club/restaurant. The empty space was previously the Stork Rooms and Crazy Horse, which have a chequered history, but supposedly back in the day played host to Billie Holiday, Marlene Dietrich, Ava

Gardner and Frank Sinatra, among others.

~

I'm off to see Tony Bennett perform. He's in his late 70s but still got it in spades. My father was often mistaken for Tony and would playfully milk it dry with the fairer sex, or any barman who was proffering a complimentary drink.

~

Jamie's taken offices above the club. It's very convenient as building work starts next week. We just need to confirm the interior designer.

~

I just had a meeting with Jamie and the supremely talented fashion designer Antony Price about the possibility of Antony designing his first-ever club interior for us. I think he's the perfect person for the job.

~

Out to Home House with Nick Rhodes for the launch party of MAC Cosmetics' charity lipstick, hosted by Pamela Anderson. It's a bit of a bun fight, so Nick's suggested we go to Tramp nightclub with a couple of his friends.

~

Nick's driver has duly delivered the four of us to the Jermyn Street institution that's still going strong since its opening in 1969, when it was the first London members' club not to enforce a formal dress code and hosted the likes of Elizabeth Taylor, Richard Burton and the Beatles. Now as Nick's guests are Bryan Ferry and Robert Downey Jr, you would think that our entrance would be gilded. Not so. The doorman has just trotted out the clichéd nightlife mantra of 'no gentlemen without ladies', before a rather embarrassing wait until the penny finally drops and another member of staff, realising exactly who these gentlemen are, whisks us off to a table, apologising profusely all the way.

~

We have ended up going with a company called Blacksheep for the club design as Jamie Lorenz thinks they'll be savvier with all the structural changes. I still think Antony would be a much cooler choice, but it's not me writing the cheque.

~

I speak to my brother about ten times a day. I speak to my sister about ten times a year. It's not that I love her any less, it's just that Skid and I share so many unnerving similarities: it's both weird and fascinating to compare notes on a daily basis. If I went into a department store and there were 100 different brands of socks, I would unknowingly come out with the exact same pair that Skid had already purchased. He is the only person in this world who I can have a frank and honest conversation with (without being sectioned a few hours later) about missing a holiday flight because I had to find a button that had dropped down the side of the sofa before I left the house. He, too, would obviously remain until the button had been found. This is going to sound completely insane to someone who doesn't suffer from these obsessions, but then there's not really any suffering. We have both turned our queer quirks into a positive lifestyle. I love having a spotlessly clean flat. I relish in knowing exactly how much money I have to the nearest penny. My wardrobe, with its suits and shirts' seasonal tonal journey from left to right, is a work of art to me, worthy of a place in a fine gallery. I wouldn't have the tins of food in my cupboard facing any other way. It's nice to know your options at a glance. And who doesn't have like with like in the fridge. Of course all the dairy products have to go on one shelf. And as for sell-by dates...

~

Now here comes the massive contradiction: my party lifestyle, where complete control is swapped for no control. I once raised this issue with my father and he replied fairly poker-faced.

'Every wobbly river bridge has a strong foundation or it would sink.'

Now, I'm not saying that my old man was Teddington's answer to Confucius, but it did strike a resonant chord with me.

~

I'm at a screening of the remastered *Born To Boogie* with Colin. Marc Bolan's son Rolan is in attendance. It's unsurprising how T. Rex's music has stood the test of time. Very strange, though, seeing Steve Currie in his element and not passed out after a few too many scotches on my mum's favourite chair in our suburban semi.

~

Drunken tomfoolery at Karen Millen the fashion designer's house party in Kent. She has a palatial pad, pond and pool. I just jumped fully clothed into the latter, forgetting my new mobile is still in my pocket and wiped out five hundred or so numbers that I was going to back up this weekend.

~

Roger Taylor's invited me to a gala performance of Queen's *We Will Rock You* tonight. I love musical theatre, much to my close friends' surprise and horror. Skid's convinced I'm a gay man trapped in a straight man's body, but surely *everyone* loves Liza Minnelli, Dirk Bogarde and John Waters.

~

Bobby Lorenz has thought of a cool name for our club: The Cuckoo Club. As in we've kicked out the stork from the Stork Club and cuckoo substitutes quite nicely for crazy, as in Crazy Horse.

~

Bobby was once one of the world's top backgammon players and made a very good living from his skill before directing his winning enthusiasm into property, the fashion industry and, finally, bars and clubs.

~

I'm stuffing my face at the launch of Nozomi restaurant in Knightsbridge, the latest venture from Marios George, who previously owned the Soho club Attica. It's contemporary Japanese cuisine and I've just consumed a sumo's body-weight of sushi and an equal amount of sake. In fact, my bloating to floating ratio is on a pretty even keel.

~

The Nashi Pear Martini has tipped the scales. It's also insulted my date, lost my cloakroom ticket, chundered on my boots and wiped out my memory.

~

The Cuckoo Club build is going very well. We had an inspiring group design meeting earlier with Blacksheep. I've suggested the Rolling Stones gate-crashing a gentlemen's club as the vibe we should go for and coined the style as 'Rock and Regal'.

~

I'm out in the depths of the English countryside with Jamie Lorenz and Dom T, who will be one of the resident DJs when we open. We're at the manufacturer's headquarters checking out Funktion One speakers, which I first discovered in Julian Stewart Lindsay's home studio. Jamie wants to hear them a little bit louder… and louder… and a touch louder… and louder. Planes are dropping from the sky and the sonic waves are making my face distort…

and louder. There go the windows… and just a tad more… and the roof.

'And how about the bass?'

~

Another club launch party. This time, Movida. It's a good opportunity to let people know about the forthcoming opening of The Cuckoo Club.

~

I'm putting a celebrity committee and founder members list together to set the foundation for the Cuckoo's prospective clientele. So far, I've pulled in Bryan Ferry, Roger Taylor, Nick Rhodes, Richard Young, Nicky Haslam, Magnus Fiennes, Alice Temperley, Dougray Scott, Guy Chambers, Isabella Blow, Jemma Kidd, Stephen Webster and Simon Mills.

~

The club is nearly finished. We are scheduled to open on the 23rd November and should hit that date, a small miracle for a new venue in the West End.

~

I'm shopping for staff outfits. Black lace dresses for the waitresses, purple shirts and black trousers for the barmen. Eight new floral shirts for me.

~

The invites have arrived. We went with a silk-covered, fold-out card and embossed metallic lettering. At £14 a pop with 800 invited guests, we're in for £11,200 before we even start licking the stamps.

~

Our PR company, Intelligent, has already garnered some sensational press, mainly focusing around the celebrity committee. The journalists all want to know exactly what the committee will be doing for Cuckoo. Not a lot. My spiel, when touting to the various celebs, was that by agreeing to be on the committee they would be treated royally when they came to the club, would receive a few honorary memberships for their friends and would have to do fuck all in return. A win/win for both sides.

~

I've been working on the musical playlist for the Cuckoo restaurant, namely blues and classic rock. We are also sticking our necks out musically with the emphasis on a cool rock 'n' roll playlist, to be worked in alongside the usual staple of dance tracks in the club area.

~

I've picked the first-ever tune to be played at The Cuckoo Club when the doors open for business. It's the symphonic version of the Rolling Stones' 'Angie'. I've also secured the services of Jackson Scott and Miles Winter Roberts as ongoing resident musicians for the early evening restaurant slot. Exquisite food and Balearic blues… not a bad mix.

~

It's launch night. 'Angie' is blaring out of the Funktion Ones. Jamie wants it louder. We've only been open for five minutes and there's already a queue stretching up to Regent Street, so our fears of no one turning up appear to be rather unfounded. I have already spotted Jools Holland, Sean Pertwee, Andrea Corr, Andrew Neil, supermodel Jodie Kidd and half of London society.

~

Dazed and Confused founder Jefferson Hack has taken to the decks with his new model girlfriend Anouck Lepère, an equally hot replacement for his ex Kate Moss. I'm knocking back our signature cocktail, the Fizzy Feathered Cuckoo, like there's no yesterday but to no effect. The adrenalin build-up over the last 48 hours is cancelling out any intoxicant, no matter how strong.

~

Skid wants to know who I have or haven't shagged in the room.
    'Really? That's punching above your weight!'

~

Disaster. The cloakroom rail has collapsed and shuffled everyone's tickets. There's now practically a punch-up going on over the rightful ownership of a Chanel black and white, bouclé, sequinned coat, and that's just between the two cloakroom attendants.

~

The feedback from last night has been universally positive. I just wish I could do it all again and fill in the blanks. I do remember that the adrenalin finally evaporated and the evening's cocktail consumption hit me in straight sets. I vaguely remember going back to an after-party at my good friend Mark Hiley's gaff. I definitely don't remember swapping clothes with a girl wearing a tutu. I do, however, remember waking up and realising the girl and my clothes had left the building.

~

Mark won't stop humming the music from *Swan Lake*, so I've answered his piss-taking melody with a bold arabesque.

~

It's the first weekend at Cuckoo and the real test of what's to come as, from tonight, the drinks are no longer complimentary. Though if you buy a magnum or so of champagne at your table, you are rewarded for your extravagance with a couple of sparkling flares attached to your bottle, which in turn is attached to a punter-proof waitress, who will deliver it to you held aloft like the pissed Pied Piper of party town. No one's going to miss your show of financial flushness, though they may question the size of your penis.

~

It's just gone midnight and it's starting to looks like Guy Fawkes Night. The magnums are coming out ten at a time and that's just to one table. One of our waitresses has been given a £500 tip just for bringing a guy a packet of cigarettes and another £50 for delivering the matches, which she forgot to bring her generous benefactor the first time around. I'm in the wrong job.

~

Marilyn Manson and his wife Dita Von Teese have come to Cuckoo for dinner. Marilyn and I are having a chat. He is actually very approachable and nothing like you would imagine. He wants to hear David Bowie's 'Be My Wife' as I think it holds some romantic significance for him and Dita. I've told him the DJ has it. He doesn't.

~

I've just dispatched a busboy to Tower Records, a stone's throw away from the club. He is back with Bowie's seminal *Low* album before Marilyn has even rejoined his table and 'Be My Wife' drops just as Marilyn's gothstar derrière hits the banquette. The DJ is playing it so loud, the level on the mixing desk has busted through red and broken back into green.

~

Jamie Lorenz has just arrived with Timo Weber, who is now Cuckoo's director of development, and Yvette Carter, our mysteriously methodical manager.

'Turn it up a bit!'

~

I've arrived late at the club tonight. A very cute girl has blocked my entrance.

'Are you here to pick someone up?'

'God, am I that obvious? I'll see how it goes, I guess.'

'Sorry, you've misunderstood me. I thought you were someone's dad.'

~

To the *Narnia* première. I remember finishing *The Lion, the Witch and the Wardrobe* in one sitting in my childhood, then spending the next few weeks slowly sawing out the back of my bedroom cupboard, much to Skid's amusement and encouragement.

~

I'm an atheist who loves Christmas. My mother was the same. She used to start her Christmas shopping in February.

~

It's a new day. It's a new year. It's another resolution spoken and broken.

~

A few days' spring sun in Tunisia. This evening, there's traditional entertainment at the hotel. She certainly has the voice of an angel… a Hells Angel.

~

My camel is refusing to budge. It's been a long, hot day in the desert and he has quite rightly had enough and is close to breaking point. I can only agree. But then five hours of repeat plays of Phil Collins's *No Jacket Required* on the guide's boombox would test the patience of any music lover. Man or beast.

~

The Toffs and Trailer Trash-themed fancy dress party at Cuckoo. I've hired a scarlet-coloured hunting jacket, complete with jodhpurs, riding boots, a top hat and a whip and added a liberal smattering of fake blood across my chops for good measure. Not a good look when you're strolling down Regent Street to cries of 'Shame on you'.

~

Life is imitating art. Thursday nights at the club have, with the help of its blue-blooded host Violet Naylor-Leyland, become aristokid central. I'm supplying the trashed element.

~

Our Thursday night has attracted the attention of the fashionistas at *Vogue* magazine, who have commissioned the world's most celebrated fashion photographer Mario Testino to shoot a feature in the club on young London and introduce the 'capital's new, bright, young things.' It's a shame they don't want a second-hand, dull, old thing for the photo shoot. I need a new passport photo.

~

The guys who run the La Dolce Vita Balls have asked me if Cuckoo fancy collaborating on a charity dinner they will be hosting in Monaco at the Salles des Etoiles. It's during the forthcoming Grand Prix and they have suggested we replicate The Cuckoo Club on-site for the VIP after-party, complete with a giant blow-up of our logo to act as the entrance.

~

Valium, ear plugs, velvet eye-mask, Nurofen, Berocca, shades. Right, that's tonight at the club sorted. Now I must pack for Monaco.

~

Wyclef Jean, of Fugees fame and founder of the Yele Haiti charity, is hosting tonight's proceedings at the Salles des Etoiles. Bono's joined him onstage for a spine-tingling duet of Bob Marley's 'Redemption Song', which raises the roof... and the donations.

~

It's time to head outside to our Johnnie Walker whisky-sponsored bar on the terrace overlooking the Mediterranean for a smoke and a joke. I've found that all of life's best discoursers are always to be found next to an ash tray.

~

Mark Fairweather, who is managing the Cuckoo bar tonight, is doing a great job for a battered man on crutches, an injury sustained on our boozy Monacoan hotel bar crawl last night. No one present at the time can remember how it happened... including Mark.

~

I've arrived home and realised that I must have picked up the wrong case from the Gatwick carousel. I'm pissed off about the inconvenience that this is going to cause me getting my case back, but also rather relieved that I wasn't stopped for a public spot check at customs and asked to explain the small bag of wacky baccy within.

~

I'm checking out Hedges & Butler, a vaulted members' club that has recently opened just around the corner from Cuckoo. Through the smoke I can just about make out one of our Cuckoo waitresses, who called in sick earlier this evening, slamming back shots. It's an enlightening experience. I was truly unaware of the healing properties of Jägermeister.

~

Off to The London Club and Bar Awards 2006. London nightlife's answer to the Oscars were founded in 1994 by Mark Armstrong, a sportive maverick who has adopted the role as the capital's nocturnal ambassador with fanatical gusto. The Cuckoo Club is nominated in the Best New Club category.

'And the winner is…'

~

It's great that we won. It's just a shame I drunkenly swapped the award for a cigarette with a passing random reveller in Leicester Square in the early hours of this morning.

~

A night hanging out with Orlando Bloom at the club. He's asked if Cuckoo can accommodate a small party he is organising around the release of the new *Pirates of the Caribbean* movie, *Dead Man's Chest*. Unfortunately we already have a booking for the night he wants, so I've offered a few other suggestions. My date keeps referring to him as the Orlando Bloom lookalike, convinced as she is that Orlando isn't actually Orlando.

~

I'm on my way home in a taxi. Orlando just called to thank me for the evening's hospitality. The date is confused as to why the 'lookalike' is carrying on the pretence.

~

Orlando's gone with the China Tang bar at The Dorchester for his drinks do. It's quite an intimate affair with Orlando, Johnny Depp, Keira Knightley (another Teddington expat) and a few others. I've got to take it easy. I'm going straight from here to Gatwick Airport to catch the 1 a.m. flight to Santorini.

'… and two Caipirinhas please.'

~

Bollocks. I've missed the plane. Luckily, they've squeezed me on to a morning flight, so I can at least grab a few hours' sleep in the departure lounge and still join Colin, who arrived yesterday, for an early evening dinner at Santorini's capital Fira's best cliff-top restaurant.

~

My mobile alarm has just woken me up. Every bone in my body aches and I've seriously crooked my neck. Still, four days lying on a beach will soon sort that out. The airport seems very busy for so early in the morning, but at least there's no queue at the departure desk.

~

There's no queue at the desk because the flight has already left. I somehow, stupidly set my alarm for 11 a.m. not 7 a.m. I will have to get the late afternoon flight.

~

There is no late afternoon flight. In fact, there are no more available flights until Friday. The day I have to come back to London.

~

'Hi Colin, It's Nick. I'm going to be a bit late for dinner, mate.'

~

Jamie Bloom's moved his girlfriend into our bachelor house, so it's time to move on.

~

After a grand tour of every overpriced dump west of Lancaster Gate, I've finally found a nice one-bedroom garden flat in Bayswater. I just need to add a few homely touches.

~

I seem to be getting rather consumed with fabric swatches, soft furnishings and trips to Homebase. My first taste of home decorating was when, aged 15, David Cuff and I dropped a tab of acid on a gloriously sunny afternoon during the annual school holidays. In my tripped-out state, I decided it would be a good idea to paint my family living room with the jeep paint I had chanced upon in the garage. I can still hear my mother's screams when she discovered my handiwork upon returning from work. I naturally professed my innocence.

'Go and look in the mirror,' was all my mother could muster between sobs.

My reflection did indeed confirm my guilt. My mother saw a wide-eyed young boy covered in army green paint. I saw a human body with a frog's head, a lizard's tongue and a telescopic neck. I had been in a fairly calm, blissful state until this confrontation. The horrors then kicked in. My sister transmuted into a Spacehopper and the lawn at the front of our house turned into a bottomless moat. My concerned mother tried to drag me to the local hospital, but I kept telling her it was too much of a risk making the crossing as I couldn't swim (I could). The hallucinations continued for a good ten hours or more until I finally conked out, along with my parents patience. This was the first and certainly the last time I ever took LSD. David Cuff, by complete contrast, had safely made it home and experienced a very pleasant, though somewhat monged-out, day.

~

I'm at a fetish club in Vauxhall. It's a monthly night with a very preternatural nature. The weird thing is, for someone who has spent as much time in nightclubs as I unashamedly have, I have very poor night-time vision, despite downing enough vitamin A to make Elmer McCollum proud. A consequence of this is that most of tonight's activities are totally lost on me, though the audio element is pretty self-explanatory and, unexpectedly, far more erotic.

~

Pink Floyd legend Dave Gilmour's daughter Sara works at Cuckoo. She has brought Axl Rose in tonight, much to everyone's delight. I just jokingly suggested to him that Guns N' Roses should do a secret gig here and he politely humoured me. Now I would love to stay and party with one of rock 'n' roll's coolest ever frontmen, but I have to catch a flight to Ibiza in less than four hours and don't want to fuck up another trip.

~

I'm scouting round the bars and clubs in Ibiza trying to find the correct venue to collaborate with The Cuckoo Club for a summer party. Jamie Lorenz just called and told me Guns N' Roses are playing at the club tonight after their Wembley Arena show. He has managed to pull the whole thing together in just two days. Guns are one of my all-time favourite bands. I'm seriously gutted not to be there.

~

I've checked every airline, but no flight will get me back in time for the show. Ironically, there's a Guns N' Roses tribute act playing in

Ibiza tonight, so I guess I'll have to settle for the musical equivalent of methadone.

~

My phone won't stop ringing. It's either people stuck outside Cuckoo trying to get in, or the lucky fuckers inside holding their phones up in the air for me to hear so they can gloat about what I'm missing. Even Dino, Cuckoo's keeper of the gates, is on the inside.

~

Skid's waiting for me at Gatwick in his new Merc. He's asked me if I've been to any good gigs recently. His phone rings. It's the newly downloaded intro to 'Sweet Child O' Mine'.

~

I've been a bit of a dog this week. I went back with a girl last night after the club finished and I'm repeating the process tonight, albeit with a different playmate. I'm off my tits, but her living room looks really familiar. So does the kitchen… and the bathroom… and her flatmate.

'Hello again, back so *soon*.'

~

The Rolling Stones at Twickenham Stadium. Keith's on fine form despite his recent brain surgery following a fall from a coconut tree. I, too, once fell out of a tree, while working in the apple orchards of a peace camp organisation in France in my teens. I made a rapid and full recovery but, bizarrely, spoke with a Jamaican accent for about two months after the accident.

~

I just joined a new online community called Facebook. I've had a bit of a root around under the supervision of Anna Horsman, Cuckoo's event manager. I don't think it will catch on.

~

Aussie rockers INXS are showcasing their new singer at the club tonight. Michael Hutchence is an impossible act to follow, but new boy JD Fortune is doing a pretty good job, all things considered. It's an unenviable task. A bit like Lyndon Johnson must have felt post-JFK.

~

Cuckoo seems to have become celeb central. In the last few weeks alone we've been graced by the likes of Christina Aguilera, Puff Daddy, David Beckham, U2, Heather Graham, Muse, Leonardo DiCaprio, Green Day, Jenson Button and Chad Smith, the Red Hot Chili Peppers drummer, who I merrily downed a few of our house shots with.

~

In fact, the ever-increasing column inches Cuckoo is now getting every day in the press seems to directly correlate with the amount of telephone calls I am now receiving asking for admittance. This can range from a considerate request for a forthcoming guest list or membership enquiry, to a rude as fuck early morning call demanding I come outside to get said person in, regardless as to whether I am in the club or, as in many frequent cases, tucked up in bed fast akip.

'Hi, yeah. Is that Nick?'

'Err… What time is it… Fuck, it's 4 a.m.'

'Yeah, that's right. You know the girlfriend of a friend of my sister's flatmate and I wanna come in.'

'You've just woken me up and we're closed now, in any case.'

'But it's my birthday and I'm with 11 friends. Can't you come down and open up?'

~

To Earls Court for the World Music Awards, hosted by Lindsay Lohan. Michael Jackson is picking up the Diamond Award in recognition of selling more than 100 million albums in the course of his career, which he probably achieved for *Thriller* alone. The crowd are expecting him to perform a couple of his greatest hits, but all he has managed is a few choruses of 'We Are the World', before toddling off. As Rihanna takes the stage, the crowd are still booing Michael. Not the most encouraging of receptions.

~

The Cuckoo's first anniversary party. I've manage to procure the musical talents of Dirty Pretty Things, featuring former Libertine Carl Barat, to help celebrate our first year. I love their debut album, *Waterloo to Anywhere*, which they're playing a hefty chunk of tonight. It's a storming set and has completely brought the house down. It's reassuring to know a kick-arse band can still move me, regardless of my advancing years and receding gums.

~

Christmas drinks in Sloane Square at Kitts, Charlie Gilkes and Duncan Stirling's new boutique venue. Club owners seem to be getting younger and younger.

~

Off to Phuket to stay with my friend Karl Putel, who is in the process of developing a few luxury resorts across Asia.

~

It's strange being back in Thailand. I'm lying on a beautiful beach, but still feel a bit edgy every time the tide draws out.

~

Steve, one of Karl's other house guests, has just popped to the local health spa for a coffee enema.

'Do you want me to bring you one back?'

'No thanks, mate, I think I'll stick to my Lipton's.'

~

Trisara resort for New Year's Eve. It's a captivating location for dinner. A mini-paradise wrapped in exotic gardens and fertile forest. Sarah, Duchess of York, has stopped for a chat with one of the guys on our table. A quick bit of London catch-up and it's all down to the beach for the countdown. As midnight strikes, a lantern for every Thai tsunami victim is launched skywards. It's both extremely touching and incredibly beautiful in a rather macabre way.

~

I'm acting on my New Year's resolution and finally looking for my own place to buy. I guess it's a sign of my age that the nesting instinct is finally kicking in. You obviously don't get an awful lot for your money in central London, so I've returned to my roots and started flat-hunting around the Richmond/Twickenham area.

~

I've made an offer on the first place I've seen: a top-floor flat in St Margarets. I knew as soon as I walked through the door I had to live here.

~

It's strange suddenly having loads of storage space. I've pretty much lived out of a bag all of my adult life. It's certainly made the OCD more manageable and given me a sense of perverse pleasure in how light I can travel. Skid shares this seemingly strange (by Western standards) attitude and is quite competitive over who can own the least. This one-downmanship has given us a lot of laughs over the years.

'I'm finally down to just one bag of stuff.'

'Me too, but I've managed to get rid of the bag.'

~

I love my new pad, but it can be a bit of a trek from The Cuckoo Club at 4 a.m. in the morning, so I've installed a sleeping bag behind the sofa in the club office for emergencies. Tonight's an emergency. The trouble is the loo is on the floor above, it's 5 a.m., I'm in the corridor just in my smalls and I've managed to lock myself out of the office... I wonder what time the cleaner arrives?

~

I'm in love. When the object of this infrequent emotion walked into the club last night I was instantly bitten and smitten. Siobhan has an Irish name but is actually Kiwi/Samoan and looks like she's just stepped straight out of *Mutiny on the Bounty*.

~

My culinary skills are pretty non-existent but Fernando Stovell, Cuckoo's master chef, has agreed to give me a crash course in contemporary cooking so that I might entertain and hopefully impress the object of my heartburn. It's probably all too little, too late, but necessity compels me to give it my best shot.

~

Dinner at Siobhan's flat in Chelsea. I'm cooking. It's a disaster. I dropped Fernando's recipe in the pasta water and now the pizza delivery guy is running late. Siobhan's told me not to worry. She's also crap in the kitchen, though does appear to be a gifted painter, as the various canvases spread around her living room testify to. She also clearly has an artist's away with the fairies temperament. Politely put, she's barking.

~

I'm in the bedroom with Siobhan and I can hear someone letting themselves into the flat.

'Who the fuck is that?'

'Oh, that's my mother. She is staying with me for a few weeks.'

Siobhan can clearly see that I feel a little uncomfortable. In fact, I feel as though I'm 13 again.

'Don't worry, I'll tell her you are one of my gay friends. It's not too much of a stretch with what you're wearing.'

~

Siobhan's mother, Asi, has a hearty conviviality, though keeps trying to set me up with Bobby or Brad and failing that... Barry.

'God, he's sooo picky.'

~

We're hosting the party tonight at Cuckoo to celebrate Oasis winning the Lifetime Achievement Award at the Brits. Liam is chatting with Kelly Jones from the Stereophonics. They want to go somewhere private to continue their conversation, so I offer to take them to the staff room. The trouble is I've had a few drinks already and can't remember the code on the door for love nor money.

'I thought so. This cunt's got nothing to do with the place.'

And then I remember...

~

Tick.

~

To the launch of Amika nightclub in Kensington. The place is chocka and there seems to be a bigger queue for the loos than the bar, though I could just be seeing double.

~

Local councils usually insist on nightclubs removing their toilet seat lids and discourage flat services in cubicles to inhibit drug use. The truth is if someone is intent on snorting something, they will do it off the bog floor if necessary... and if that's not flat then...

~

A private view of eminent society and showbiz photographer Richard Young's highly prized portraits. Richard started his career in the early 70s when his shots of John Paul Getty III, recently released from his Italian kidnappers, albeit missing an ear that had been sent to his father to speed up ransom negotiations, were purchased by the *Evening Standard*. Richard then further made his name with *Ritz Magazine*, before photographing everyone from the Sex Pistols to Nelson Mandela, in an illustrious career that has so far spanned 33 years. His laid-back approach ensures he captures his subjects in a relaxed manner in fairly uncomfortable surroundings. He's as much an ubiquitous presence on the London party scene as champagne, Rennies and me.

~

It's early evening at Cuckoo. A singer called Anjani Thomas is playing a showcase here tonight. I'm curious and want to check her out, so I'm killing time chatting with Tav, one of our barmen, while he methodically slices up limes. An elderly guy with a Canadian accent is hovering around the finger nosh that's plated up and cellophaned ready for tonight's guests. He's asked me very gingerly if he can make a start on the grub. I've no idea who he is but I'm guessing he has something to do with tonight's gig.

'Sure, buddy... tuck in. I don't think anyone will notice.'

Tav's laughing.

'Do you know who that fucking is, Nick?'

'I've no idea at all. Why, who is it?'

'Leonard Cohen.'

'Really? As in one of the greatest and most famous singer/songwriters of all time?'

'Hallelujah.'

~

Another nightclub opening. This time Maddox club, on the site of the old Noble Rot. They have an enclosed outside space, which is a huge plus-point for them with the new smoking ban coming in to effect in a few months' time. I cannot imagine what it will be like having to step out into the cold for a fag, though I guess it will help me cut down to two packs a day… so that's good.

~

A call from my friend Jonathan Boreham, who owns a brand sponsorship/product placement company. He mainly specialises in the film industry and wants to know if The Cuckoo Club would be interested in running the cocktail bars on board a 237-foot luxury yacht, for a charity party during the Cannes Film Festival. Now, let me think for half a second.

'Oh, ok then.'

'And can you supply a band?'

'Sure. What's the charity?'

'Not On Our Watch. It's George Clooney's charity to help end genocide in the Darfur region of the Sudan. He'll be hosting, of course, with other stars of his latest movie, *Ocean's Thirteen*, attending. That's Brad Pitt, Matt Damon, Andy Garcia and Don Cheadle. *OK! Magazine* are sponsoring it… Should be a good one.'

~

I'm just calling Miles Winter Roberts, our resident singer/songwriter at Cuckoo.

'Hi mate, it's Nick. Do you want the good news or the bad news?'

'The good news.'

'The good news is you're performing for George Clooney and friends on the *RM Elegant* in Cap d'Antibes next week.'

'And the bad news?'

'I'm playing bass.'

~

It's soundcheck time. The scorching sun is beating down on my back, while the ice-cold lager goes to work on my tonsils and loosens my fingers. It's one of those majestic moments in life that you want to freeze in time forever. I decided against bringing my bass guitar in the end as I couldn't be arsed to lug it about. It weighs a ton. Instead, I've brought some bongos and a light stand I picked up from a drum store on the way to the airport. So it's not just a soundcheck, it's also our first-ever rehearsal. Still, at least the gig is low-key.

~

Bad news for Miles and me. *OK! Magazine* are paying a whopping amount of dollar for exclusive rights to the party, so the numerous amount of stars in attendance are not allowed up on deck to see us in case they get papped by a rogue photographer on shore with a long lens. At least the crew of the massive yacht moored alongside us are appreciating our performance. I recognise the name… How weird. It's my old friend David Gosling's father Donald's floating fantasy.

~

OK! Publisher Richard Desmond has joined in on drums. It's getting more surreal by the second.

~

'You're great on the bongos. How long have you been playing?'
   'Since this afternoon or thereabouts.'
   'God, I love British humour.'

~

I've come down a deck or two to mingle with Tinseltown's finest and assert some quality control over the Cuckoo cocktails. It's a massive cliché but celebrities are always much shorter in real life than you can ever possibly imagine. Another cliché is that superstars radiate a kind of ethereal charisma. Both of these I have to say apply in equal measure to Captain Clooney, he of the good ship star-struck.

~

My text update to Skid has been rudely interrupted by one of *OK!*'s security guys, who, despite my protestations, is convinced I'm trying to take a sneaky snap and wants me to leave the party. Miles thinks it hilarious, as he is well aware that my technophobia ensures that I wouldn't know how to use the camera on my phone, even if I so desired. Even texting for me is a struggle.

'You can stay, but I'll be watching you.'

'That's great. We will be on again in ten minutes.'

~

It's 3 a.m. There's not a taxi to be had in 100-mile radius and Brad's offer of a lift in his limo was not forthcoming. It looks like Miles and my glittering gala of an evening has come to a sobering halt. Oh, hold on… help is at hand.

~

'Thanks for the lift, guys, you're legends.'

~

Oh shit, I've left my bongos in the back of the dustcart.

~

My Mediterranean percussive foray has reawakened a dormant musical passion in me for performing. I think I've finally found my instrument, or instruments. I just need a mini black cabasa to complete my set-up and I'm good to go.

~

I'm thoroughly basking in my new Thursday night residency at The Cuckoo Club with Miles.

'Has anyone seen my maracas?'

~

David Schwimmer is in the club tonight. I think he might be seeing one of our waitresses, Zoe, who just introduced me to him. I then in turn, 'and it doesn't get any more cringey', to quote Miles, introduced him to Siobhan as Ross.

'I bet the poor sod gets that twice a night, five times a week.'

~

A weekend away on the Fashion TV boat in the south of France. I don't have the best sea legs, so it's a joyous relief that we have taken the tender to Nikki Beach in St Tropez, which today is like London clubland-on-sea with prices to match, except here I don't have a pretty much unlimited, complimentary tab.

~

Dinner with Alan McGee, the Creation Records founder, who among many acts of musical genius has signed or managed The Jesus and Mary Chain, Primal Scream and Oasis, three of my top 20, all-time favourite bands. We are bringing his club night Death Disco to The Cuckoo Club for a *Later with*-style TV show to be broadcast by Rockworld TV. Alan still seems as passionate as ever about music and the old and breaking talent to be featured in the show. We've agreed to film the first episode in a couple of weeks' time.

~

A beautiful sunny day. I'm in the China White enclosure at the Cartier International Polo at Windsor with Siobhan, Anshuman

Mishra and his buddy, cricket legend Brian Lara. It's a heady mix of 'cash, brash and gash', to quote Skid, who's just joined us, having dropped off one of his multimillionaire clients at the wrong entrance.

~

The polo is in full swing but it's not of great interest to me. I'm far keener on the post-polo activities. The first and only time I rode on a horse it bolted while I was still adjusting the stirrups, while precariously hanging down from the saddle. I managed to hold on for dear life under its belly for a few minutes that felt like a lifetime, until it got tired of my girly screams and came to an abrupt halt. To add to the embarrassment, I was told that my ride was normally used to teach kiddies, on account of its gentle nature.

'And technically it's a pony, not a horse.'

~

The Death Disco TV series is going great guns. Mark Sloper, the director, has got right into the spirits and things. We've already had indie supergroup the Chavs, The Charlatans, Glasvegas and Enter Shikari tread the Cuckoo stage. Tonight it's Oregon's fearless and finest, The Dandy Warhols.

~

I partied with Siobhan and the Dandies post-gig to ten past bacon and eggs. Their crazily charismatic singer Courtney Taylor-Taylor sure likes to party. I'm hanging by a thread now, but unfortunately the taxi delivering me to my 15-tog is stuck in morning rush-hour traffic and the cab is stuttering like a politician at an expenses enquiry.

~

An invite to Pattie Boyd's biography launch tonight. She was apparently the inspiration for both Eric Clapton's 'Wonderful

Tonight' and George Harrison's 'Something'. I had dinner with George's son Dhani at Cuckoo quite soon after we opened and he actually looks more like George Harrison than George Harrison. It's quite freaky. I've actually never been much of a Beatles fan, but do rate George's solo stuff. I also love the quote attributed to John Lennon, but apparently spawned from the pen of the American writer Allen Saunders: 'Life is what happens to us while we are making other plans.'

~

I'm at the party to launch The Valmont Club. I remember coming to this site in one of its previous incarnations, taking a pee in the urinal and then noticing to my horror that it had gone straight through the stained porcelain trough on to my new suede loafers.

~

Yet another launch of a new club called Maya, then on to Pangaea for a quick Moscow Mule, where I offer the valet my Oyster Card and finally to Cuckoo for a slow gin with Guy Chambers, who is going to play a show here in a few weeks.

~

'Coffee?'

My eyelids feel like they've been superglued to my eyeballs. I'm in my office (again). It's the middle of the night. What's Hilary, Cuckoo's financial director, doing here?

'What are you doing here?'

'Working. What are you doing here?'

'I just came up for a quick disco nap. I better get back down. I've still got a few friends at my table.'

'What time do you think it is, Nick?'

'I don't know… 2 a.m.?'

'Try 1 p.m.'

~

My body seems to now take about a week to recover from a session, whereas in the past I use to boast immortality, or that I'd at least conquered sleep. Clocking my reflection this morning, I've noticed that my laughter lines are splitting their sides and my posture's returning to the womb. I used one of Colin's guest gym passes last week and his hefty trainer told me I have the flexibility of a gingerbread man. Mind you, although I can't touch my toes at least I can still see them.

~

It's the second birthday party for The Cuckoo Club. Sadie Frost is on the decks. I'm on the wagon. My quilt is calling.

~

Off to the Caribbean. Siobhan's mother is a ship's doctor so we're joining her on her latest cruise, a two-week whisk around six tourist-tagged islands. I'm hoping the weather holds and Mother Nature's not planning any further surprises for me.

~

Christmas day in Miami, our departure port tomorrow. I'm in architectural heaven with my love of art deco, a passion picked up from my grandfather George. It's incredibly sunny today, so the only hint of festive joy is coming from Boney M, Johnny Mathis and Wham on my iPod and the Elvis snow globe I've picked up from a seafront tourist shop: some yang to balance the yin.

~

With the exception of Siobhan, who is 20 years my junior, I'm probably the youngest person on the cruise and certainly the slimmest. It's all very cheesy but then I love cheese. Ballroom dancing, musical theatre, quiz nights. I'm in promenade postcard heaven. There's even a club for 'Friends of Dorothy', Asi, Siobhan's mother, keeps joking, should I fancy it.

~

We've just docked at our third island in as many days. With only a day on each they tend to rather blend into one. I think we're on Aruba but it could well be Bermuda.

~

Two minutes in the sun and I turn black, I'm certainly my mother's son. Skid, on the other hand, inherited my father's pale skin and blue eyes so frazzles to a nice shade of salmon pink under UV. He is always telling me that the guy who lived below us in the police flats where I was born had exactly my colouring, and nose and physique…

~

Dominica, our final island before heading back to Miami. A leisurely afternoon shopping for Siobhan and a spot of sunbathing for me. It's audio bliss, *The Best of King Tubby* bouncing out of the beach bar's battered speakers, with the bass so deep it cannot fail to both liberate your inner dread and loosen your bowels. The barman tells me he's on the ganja diet.

'Last week, I lost three days.'

~

Much excitement at Cuckoo tonight as Princes William and Harry have dropped by. I just showed Harry around the joint and he exuberantly showed his thanks by putting me in a headlock. William was somewhat more restrained with a courtly handshake.

~

Princess Diana died on my birthday. I was on a remote Greek island called Patmos at the time, celebrating reaching 35, so missed all the mass public hysteria. The powers that be certainly work in most mysterious ways. I'm by no means a conspiracy theorist, but did spend an unusual evening once sharing cocoa with a few guys from an army regiment that does not exist on paper. They were supposed to be honing their survival skills (on a then girlfriend's father's rugged estate), before being dropped prematurely into a country we later went to war with. The lure of a hot drink and a rich tea finger proved too much for them, however, which was strange, as here were guys who had remained unfazed when electrodes were clipped to their nuts in a past exercise, just as a warm-up.

~

To celebrity photographer Dave Benett's 50th birthday party. I've probably seen Dave out and about at least twice a week for the last 15 years. If he is not at an event I attend, I immediately start worrying that there must be a better party on somewhere else that I somehow don't know about… There inevitably is.

~

Off to New York for a few days, courtesy of Belvedere Vodka, which is hosting a dinner and party with Jade Jagger to publicise the Jagger Dagger, a gem-encrusted sword, for use as an exclusive tableside ice-picking service in selected nightclubs.

~

An eternity to clear customs. How strange that being a director of a nightclub would necessitate such a thorough search. Still, I suppose at least I can give the Senokot a miss tonight.

~

The party in an old church on the Lower East Side, that's been tarted up for the occasion, is in full swing. I've bolted down dinner but I am taking it easy on the booze as I don't want to feel too squiffy for my scheduled morning helicopter flight over Manhattan. A shard of ice striking me right on the snout, sent flying from an over-jealous swordsman, is probably my signal to head home so I take my leave, passing a buoyant Harvey Weinstein on the way out.

~

The view from the helicopter is something else. The New York skyline takes me back to all my favourite New York-set cops shows that I watched while growing up in the suburbs, while dreaming of neon-lit, pollution-choked cities yet to be explored, wrapped conspiratorially and cosily in my Starsky cardigan, a lopsided birthday present from my mother and possibly the genesis of my future OCD.

~

I'm at the Box club, a risqué, vaudevillian 'Theatre of Varieties' in downtown Manhattan run by Simon Hammerstein, grandson of the legendary Oscar Hammerstein. Jade and Mick Jagger have joined the table next to mine, just in time for the twisted twin show, one of many acts robustly pounding the stage tonight for our delight and delectation. It's all very Weimar-era Berlin in its content and quite amusing, but the shock element of the various acts at our disposal wears off surprisingly quickly. Definitely a case of more is less, to my seasoned eyes.

~

A quick lunch before heading to the airport. I bumped into David Schwimmer on my way into the restaurant. I have not seen him since my faux pas at The Cuckoo Club but he was suitably friendly and still dating Zoe, by all accounts.

~

The London Club and Bar Awards 2008. It's quite an interesting concept: an awards *dinner* for nightlife's bacchanalian movers and shakers. Needless to say, not a huge amount of food is consumed at the event, which is rather strange considering the mass of people licking their lips. I'm up for the Sexiest Host Award.

~

It's 3 a.m. and a cab home is proving elusive. Siobhan sensibly left hours ago. It's pissing with rain, so I am using my award as a makeshift umbrella. I'm soaked to the bone and feel about as sexy as a weary eunuch with a splitting headache and a fresh outbreak of herpes.

~

Dinner at Cuckoo with two of my musical heroes. Paul Cook and Steve Jones have just reformed the Sex Pistols with the original line-up to play at The Isle of Wight Festival. I first met Paul when we were trying to secure the rights to 'Holidays in the Sun' for the *Brothers* soundtrack. Steve is teetotal these days, though Paul is still up for a drink or two.

~

The cultural significance of the Sex Pistols can never be totally understood unless you were lucky enough to be in your teens in the mid-to-late 70s. They literally changed everything almost overnight on the back of their infamous Bill Grundy interview. Music, fashion, publishing... I remember going into my local pet shop the day following Grundy's fall from grace, after first ditching my disco/casual outfit of copper-topped boots, mohair jumper and red peg trousers and trying on my first dog collar (an intrinsic part of punk fashion and a rites of passage for me), with Skid at my side for moral support.

'This one's too big for him. You got anything for a toy poodle?'

~

I'm back in Ibiza to organise a Cuckoo party in conjunction with Pussy energy drink (who want to move into the Ibizan market) at Bo Bendtsen's lavish holiday home overlooking the port. Tonight I'm out on the hunt for two beguiling cross-dressers to act as door whores.

~

I found a couple of beauties. They must be about nine foot tall in heels and headdresses and are proving an alluring hit with the arriving guests. The sun has just barely set, but there must already be a good 100 people here chilling out to Jackson Scott's live flamenco set.

~

The party has been a great success, but seems to be winding down. It's time to hit the old town and its myriad of late-night bars.

~

I've run into an old acquaintance.
    'Here, try this.'
    I've taken a big swig.
    'I can't taste the booze, just the orange juice.'
    'Well, you wouldn't. Give it five minutes.'
    'Give what five minutes?'
    'The MDMA.'

~

I've finally come down. Not in a bad way. I just feel a lot less 'Kumbayah My Lord'. I sure made a lot of new friends last night. The sun is already scorching, so it seems pointless going to bed. Maybe I'll join Jackson on the nearby island of Formentera today, as he suggested at the party.

~

We have found a completely deserted stretch of white sand to crash out on. What a contrast to the madness of Ibiza. Fresh bread and crispy whitebait with aioli for brunch, picnic style, all washed down with a bottle of the local plonk. The perfect recovery package. I'm completely knackered and could sleep for a week. Time for the all-over tan.

'Speak to you in about eight hours, then, mate.'

'Yeah. Sweet dreams.'

~

I've woken to a cool breeze and a blazing body. I don't normally burn, but then I usually remember to slap on the Factor 8. I've even scorched the soles of my feet. I'm actually radiating. Thank God a strategically placed bandana has prevented my pecker from being deep fried and permanently retired.

~

Back at the villa. Even the iced bath is failing to put out the fire. My barbecued torso will no doubt turn a nice shade of mahogany… in about nine months.

~

Off with Colin to see the reunited Blow Monkeys play. A blast from the past. The pouting, poetical percussionist Mickey Finn joined these guys briefly post T. Rex in what was a very natural fit, with the Monkey's vocalist Dr. Robert and Marc Bolan both exuding a very similar star quality.

~

A call from a gruff-sounding Russian guy called Vladimir. He wants to know if I would like to meet him and a few of his associates to discuss opening a new club in Mayfair. I'm perfectly happy at Cuckoo, but a tad curious, so have agreed to a rendezvous.

~

Vladimir's associates are all Russian, all domiciled in the UK and all called Andrey. They have taken on the shell of a five-storey Georgian townhouse and need someone to conceptualise, create and run a nightclub, cocktail bar and 30-cover restaurant, with two private dining rooms thrown into the mix. They are offering a fine salary and a decent percentage of equity in the place. I've said I'll sleep on it and let them know.

~

I actually didn't sleep a wink, as my brain would not switch off after the many hours spent weighing up the pros and cons.

~

The pros have come out on top. Time to fly the coop.

~

I've been inspired by Moorish architecture with its rich colour palate for the design of the club, with additional influences coming from 50s Vegas and David Lynch's *Wild at Heart* movie. That means lots of bold earth colours for the floors and walls, contrasting with lurid faux skins – stingray, ostrich and snake for the upholstery – and copper and antique brass metallic finishes for the paintwork. Subtle it's not. Flamboyant it certainly is. For the name, I've decided on Molton House as we are in South Molton Street and the logo will feature a keyhole and peacock feathers, representing a secret passage into another world à la Alice in Wonderland.

~

The builders have uncovered a small hidden room behind the first-floor fireplace, so I've decided on a sunken DJ booth, after my first suggestion of a shark tank was overruled as the weight load would be too great. So far I've chosen near on 80 different finishes and fabrics. This is not going to be cheap. I've been told the budget is 'Just get it finished.'

~

It's been a mega-stressful five-month build, with probably a month still to go. It's much scarier when the final buck stops with you and a massive wad of someone else's money is being spent on *your* vision.

~

The vision has been realised, but I am well aware that the final look is very Marmite in its 'love it or hate it' way. The cocktail bar is camper than Christmas, the restaurant thrilled and feathered to the max and the private dining rooms are very bordello-esque in their feel. The dance floor has carnival lights and my opera, musical theatre and Motown music policy in the bar has been described as 'gutsy'. Personally, I love it.

~

Skid's daughter Clio has moved to London, so I've given her a waitressing job at the club. I must tell her to stop calling me Uncle Nick. It makes me feel about 46.

~

The staff and staff outfits are signed off. The invite, a metal key in an engraved box, is ready to go. I just need to find a snakeskin suit and matching boots for the launch.

~

To Mahiki for a catch-up drink with Colin. I've hardly seen him since the whole Molton House thing started. I have an extremely important meeting first thing tomorrow with the Andreys and the council, so I'm in first gear tonight. I figure if I stick to just one of Mahiki's famous Treasure Chests, a swashbuckling cocktail if ever there was one, I can grab a bite to eat and still be tucked up in bed by 10 p.m.

~

I don't normally party in east London, but it seemed like a good idea after the third Treasure Chest. Colin's even drunker than me and that takes some serious drinking.

'I'm going to head home, Col, I've gotta make this 9 a.m. meeting.'

'Good luck. It's 8.30 a.m. now.'

~

I haven't got a clue where I am. I'm hoping Skid can come to my rescue and deliver me to Molton House.

'Where are you, mate?'

'I've no idea.'

'Go and look at a street sign.'

'Alderney Road, E1.'

'See you in 20, stay put.'

'Thanks a million, bro. I owe you big time.'

~

9.20 a.m. That's not too bad. A couple of Red Bulls and a gallon of water and I'll be fine. I just need to grab Mark, our general manager, for some moral support.

'I need you to cover my back, buddy.'

'Sure. Here, have a mint. You reek.'

~

We're all in my office. The three Andreys, a couple of guys from the council and Mark. I'm struggling to keep my eyes open, fighting to keep the sick from breaking cover from my tonsils and desperately trying to make sense of all the paperwork being passed around.

~

I've woken up with a start. My office is empty. I'd better go and find Mark.

~

'Hi mate. What happened?'
'Well you pretty much fell asleep after the introductions to the blokes from the council. If that wasn't bad enough, you then snored like a trooper through the whole meeting. At least they know the club is in safe hands.'
'At least indeed. I better go and apologise to the Andreys.'
'You better.'

~

'I'm really sorry guys, I, erm...'
'Nick... we're Russian, no big deal.'

~

Two weeks to go until the opening. Tonight we are hosting Duran Duran singer Simon Le Bon's 50th birthday dinner. The venue is way off being ready, but I've improvised with drapes, flowers and scented candles, the candles' main purpose being to mask the prevalent smell of paint.

~

Simon and his lovely wife Yasmin seem fairly happy, though a few of his guests look in danger of passing out from the noxious fumes. At least the decor and the nosh are getting a big thumbs-up.

~

It's all back to Simon's to continue the party and breathe some fresh air.

~

Molton House launch night. The club is still not finished, but that's par for the course in clubland. It's not quite a hard-hat scenario, but the snagging list is still as long as the queue of guests outside waiting patiently for Dave Doyle, the council's fire officer, to sign off the building so we can open the doors.

~

We are absolutely rammed. So full, in fact, that I've escaped with Blur's bassist Alex James on to the roof. It's even getting crowded up here. I think I may have sent out a few too many invites. It's time to move downstairs and check out the Cherry Blossom Bellinis.

~

I can just make out T4's Steve Jones, *Control* director Anton Corbijn and Dan Macmillan through the throng. I'm wondering if the new floor can take the weight, while a barrage of texts are still coming through from friends asking if they can bring extra guests.

~

The DJ has just dropped The Sweet's 'Ballroom Blitz', the first record I ever bought in 1973. Colin's turned up dressed like a Harlem pimp. He says I look like I've been swallowed by an anaconda.

~

I've worn out the snooze button on my alarm. It's something p.m., but I can at least make out daylight through my blinds so I know at least I haven't completely missed the day. I've fired up the laptop and propped it on a pillow. Happy days! There's lots of positive feedback about the club online. One reviewer has described it as a 'Ridiculously flamboyant and decadent haunt for those who don't have to worry about downsizing their nights out.' That will do me.

~

To Richmond registry office. I'm getting married today. Skid thinks it's an end of an era. To me, it's business as usual. Neither Siobhan nor I are the 2.4 stereotypes. In fact my post-wedding schedule is looking even more hectic on the social side, what with Molton House and everything, than at any other time in my life and Siobhan is certainly not a stay-at-home bride.

~

Al Martino's 'Speak Softly Love' is Siobhan's cue. It's a right old choker. She knocked up her satin and antique lace wedding dress in a few days, with no previous training, and looks stunning.

~

'I do.'

~

A post-wedding reception at Molton House. Colin is in the throes of a hilarious best man's speech. There's a dramatic pause before he delivers the punchline…

'Can you please evacuate the building, can you please evacuate the building.'

That's not the punchline, that's the fire alarm going off with split-second comic timing.

~

The first dance. Keely Smith's version of 'I Can't Help Falling in Love with You'. There's not a dry eye in the place, but that's probably a collective reaction to the ammonium phosphate from the fire extinguishers.

~

To Vienna for my honeymoon. I can't get the bloody Ultravox song out of my head. Tonight we are having dinner in a cellar restaurant that the current owner tells me has been graced by the presence of Mozart, Napoleon and Hitler.

'But not all on the same night, you understand.'

~

The bridal suite has a bridal kit. Cherry lube, a bottle of fizz and a New Testament bible. All that you obviously need for a long and successful marriage in Austria.

~

Back to work with a biblical enthusiasm for the devil's deeds.

~

A glam.com party at Molton House tonight. Carl Barat has just dedicated 'Bang Bang You're Dead' to me, ending his set of perfectly crafted, visceral tales. He has recently been diagnosed with pancreatitis, so is a little overjoyed when I tell him that I also have suffered with it but have had no recurrent attack in more than seven years.

'Well, I'll drink to that.'

~

Cocktails with my table manager Alastair Gallichan at Jalouse, a new nightclub that has just opened around the corner from Molton House in Hanover Square. He has started seeing my niece Clio. Clubland tends to be very socially contained as people outside of it tend to work completely different hours. When I've dated 9-to-5ers in the past, I would regularly be getting in as they were getting up to go to work.

~

Princesses Beatrice and Eugenie popped into the club tonight, as did England cricket bad boy Kevin Pietersen with his wife, ex-

Liberty X singer Jessica Taylor, and a couple of the England rugby squad. I first met Kevin at The Cuckoo Club where he was trading cricket stories with Mick Jagger, a self-confessed cricket fanatic. He is a very cool, laid-back guy and has cleverly brought a swaggering rock 'n' roll attitude to a traditionally stick-in-the-mud sport. Cue the sponsorship deals.

~

Kevin's back. This time with England and Chelsea football icon, Frank Lampard. I've just shown Frank the rudiments of bongo playing (in the land of the blind and all that), and he has cordially signed a few odds and sods for my nephew Piers, an avid Chelsea fan despite growing up and living in Sydney.

~

Gavin and Stacey's Mathew Horne is guest DJ in the club tonight for the Estethica party. I've seen other celebrity DJs bring in a pre-mixed set (compiled by a DJ mate) and then pretend to mix, without actually troubling the Allen and Heath's in any way whatsoever. Nice work if you can get it.

~

A preview screening in the club tonight for Paris Hilton's *British Best Friend* TV show. Paris seems to me to be fairly uninterested in her new BBFs, who are all in attendance. Richard Young has just taken a snap of the two of us. I can hear her thinking 'Who the fuck am I being photographed with?'

'Perhaps you should tell her that you're the guy who has given her the venue for free tonight.'

~

It goes without saying that most celebrities expect everything to be complimentary. It also goes without saying that the right celebrity pictured in your venue translates to longer queues at your door after the glossies have hit the newsstands.

~

Didier Drogba's at the bar. Aussie Blue Piers is going to love his uncle's next package.

~

I finished my consultancy with *Entertainment News* today after an 11-year run, having co-founded it in 1998. I've pretty much stopped going to any event outside of Molton House, which is all time-consuming. The goody bag drawer has never looked so empty.

~

Dinner with my friend Akashia Hoosein, who found us our chef, and former conservative MP Michael Portillo. He is an unlikely guest in clubland, but fine and spirited company nevertheless. This is why I love what I do. The sheer random nature of who you might break bread with on any given evening.

~

I'm off to the MTV Europe Music Awards in Liverpool with the Xlantic Music Group and British American Tobacco. Katy Perry and Jared Leto are hosting the ceremony and there's a pick and mix line-up of acts performing, including Take That, The Killers, Kid Rock, Pink and Duffy.

~

It's showtime. Most awards ceremonies tend to drag on forever and you soon become far more painfully aware of how much your arse is aching in the narrow bucket seats, than how great the act performing on stage is. Tonight is an exception. It's whizzed by quicker than your average reality star's 15 seconds of fame.

~

I've joined the herd shuffling towards the after-party. It's funny being a bleating sheep after my nightly shepherding at the club. It certainly makes me appreciate my position and the gleeful abuse I give it.

~

A room service breakfast. I love hotels. Most people I know when they check in somewhere, spread the contents of their bulging suitcase all over their room to make it feel more homely. I'm the exact opposite. I try and make my flat look as much like a hotel as humanly possible, though Skid reckons the Do Not Disturb sign and the mini-bar is taking it too far.

~

INXS founder Andrew Farriss has popped in to Molton House. I haven't seen him since his gig at Cuckoo. He is a big tequila fan, so we're trying out a few new brands. I've told my niece Clio that if I mention anything about popping over to Paris she must close the bar immediately and lock me in my office.

~

I've woken up in the UK, which is a relief as tonight I'm having dinner with Rockworld's Andy Loveday and his mate Danny Dyer, who I've partied with on a few occasions and always needed a week to recover from the experience. I'd better call my event manager and tell her to cancel all my appointments for the next two days… Better make it three.

~

Sorry, four.

~

To a gala performance of *Priscilla, Queen of the Desert* with Siobhan and her mother Asi. I love the stage production even more so than the film. Asi wants to know if there is a lock on the closet.

~

My first-ever experience of cocks in frocks was watching my father Tom dolled up as Cinderella in the annual police pantomime. He was a natural. In his late teens he had actually been Anthony Newley's understudy for some production or other, but had been dissuaded from a career treading the boards by his father, who thought it far too 'poncy'.

~

An email from my friend Jane Owen who lives in Los Angeles. Can I show her friend, the actor Jason Segel, who is here to shoot *Gulliver's Travels*, the night sites of London? Jason starred in *Knocked Up* and wrote and starred in *Forgetting Sarah Marshall*, but I'd not actually put a face to a name until he turned up at Molton House tonight. He seems pretty affable and seemingly unstarry, so post-dinner it's straight to my table for champagne and shots.

~

Jason's come back for more punishment. I've promised to take him on a club crawl tonight. So far we have had a swift one in Molton House, The Century Club, Cuckoo and now Pigalle. He is very popular with the ladies, so much so that I'm starting to feel fairly invisible. An impossible task for Jason for as well as being instantly recognisable, he also towers above me and I'm 6 foot 1.

~

We've ended up at a party on the roof terrace of my friend Mark Fuller's new £10 million boutique hotel, Sanctum Soho. Mark's partners manage Iron Maiden and the hotel reflects this with its rock 'n' roll attitude, rooftop hydro spa and stacks of Marshall amplifiers on the outside terrace.

~

One of the revellers we picked up on route has just relocated her
supper. I can't believe that so much puke has come out of such
a tiny frame. It's rather killed the vibe, though it's good to see it
hasn't killed hers, as she's just tried to order another round of
sambucas from the bemused barman, globules of sick still running
down her chin.

~

My mate Patrick Deane has brought Kevin Spacey into Molton
House tonight. Kevin wants to smoke, but doesn't particularly
want to puff away on the pavement in full view of the hovering
paparazzi. I've suggested we can have a sneaky fag in my office,
so here I am exchanging pleasantries with a triple A-list star over a
packet of 20 Lights. I'm always telling Skid that non-smokers miss
out on all the fun.

'And the cancer, and the bad breath, and the yellow fingers and
the…'

~

It's that time of year again. The London Club and Bar Awards 2009
at the Riverbank Plaza Hotel. Molton House is in the running for
the Best Members' Club. It's a bitter-sweet night for me, as it follows
another massive row with the Andreys, Molton House's backers,
who I've not been seeing eye to eye with for quite some time.

~

Molton House won. I've quit. Life's too short.

~

The Lifetime Achievement Award went to Rusty Egan tonight.

Rusty was instrumental in setting up The Blitz Club with Steve Strange and then The Camden Palace, which for a while successfully relocated cool clubbing away from central London and even further away from Richmond, where I was then living. Amphetamine sulphate, known as whizz, was the drug of choice in this era and dutifully sped up the arrival time of your morning Tube back to suburbia.

~

A week in Florence with Siobhan to recharge. I'm completely burned out. It's so nice to be tootling from one gallery to the next without a care in the world, while Siobhan sketches and photographs anything and everything that doesn't move.

~

I've started to write my autobiography. It's a purgative process. A way to make sense of the craziness of spending the last 32 years chasing my tale.

~

Jamie Bloom has asked me to consult on his new venture, a pool bar in Earls Court to be called Miss Q's. It's a great space with 400 capacity over one floor, right on the main drag, with an additional room for private parties. I've suggested we add a live music element and further nail our colours to the mast, with the tagline 'Sex, Rugs and Rock 'n' Roll' pertaining to the Persian rugs under every pool table.

~

Paul Daly, the award-winning interior designer, has conceived and styled Miss Q's along the lines of an American dive bar and I've now added a Rogues of Rock gallery. I just need to find a cool poster of Keith Moon and it will be complete. He is in noble and notorious company alongside the likes of Shane MacGowan, The Cramps,

Syd Barrett, Jerry Lee Lewis, Gene Vincent, Jim Morrison, the New York Dolls, Nick Cave and err… George Formby. Obviously, some more roguish than others.

~

We launch tonight. I've become quite a pool shark over the last few months of the build and Jamie's son Eddy has just presented me with my own heavily lacquered, inscribed pool cue.

'If you can't pot the pink, then brown's right there to sink.' Charming.

~

The King has taken the stage. This pretender to the throne is not dear Elvis, but James Brown, an Irish, ex-postman, Presley sound-alike who dominated my decks for a few months with his debut album of covers of dead rock stars' songs: *Gravelands*. He's just finished an awesome set with Nirvana's 'Come As You Are'.

~

James has left the building.

~

It's the public opening and our first night of trading with The Hotrats, featuring Gaz Coombes and Danny Goffey of Supergrass fame, playing live. Danny has to play an electronic drum kit because of our noise restrictions. He sounds like he's playing underwater, but it's an inspired set nevertheless and makes me realise how great it is to be back in a live music environment.

~

Birthday drinks for Roger Taylor's sassy girlfriend, Sarina. Roger's bandmate Brian May has just checked out the Miss Q's Rogues gallery and it turns out he is a huge fan of… George Formby.

~

Skid is another Formby fan and he, too, is quite a dab hand on the old mini banjolele. Apparently, it's not the size of your instrument, it's how you make it sing that counts.

~

Alex Proud has added yet another venue to his portfolio of galleries and music venues with Proud Cabaret, a recently opened, burlesque-style restaurant and bar in the City. It's modelled on a 1920s speakeasy with entertainment and a music policy to match. It has an open kitchen and I've just spotted my old Molton House chef Finley Logan slaving away, so I know the nosh is going to be good tonight.

~

Finley's certainly ended up cooking in a very cool place, but in quite a sterile area, though there is a continued trend of former West End punters now heading to the City and further east in search of their kicks and value for money, so Alex has obviously made a smart move.

~

I'm west London to the core, though my roots on my mother's side are all in the East End. Her grandfather, Ernest Lange, actually owned a pub in Carr Street in Limehouse, though he sadly took his own life in the saloon bar one afternoon, distraught over the death of his son from pneumonia.

~

A charity night at Miss Q's hosted by Tess Daly for my dear friend Ludka, who is bravely fighting cancer. Guy Chambers is closing the evening with a rendition of the Robbie Williams classic 'Angels', which he co-wrote. I've suggested that we silent-auction the performance for a guest vocalist.

~

It's nearing the end of the night and my bid is the highest. I can't carry a tune to save my life, so I've opted to play bongos instead. Now 'Angels' is not a ditty that lends itself to bongos and I'm three drinks past tipsy, so my performance is, to say the very least, a tad embarrassing. Still it's all for a great cause, so no matter.

~

Guy has generously described my effort as a 'different take on conventional percussion'.

~

A friend's stag do in Miss Q's private room. The stripper and I have locked eyes. Here she comes, straight towards me. There go my glasses… Well, that's an interesting new home for them.

~

'Anyone got a lens cloth?'

~

A reunion gig with Miles Winter Roberts on the Earls Court Festival's open air stage. Miles has suggested we cover 'Angels' as an encore.

'Ha fucking ha.'

~

The Miss Q's burgers are starting to take their toll. I'm turning from an Elvis fan into an Elvis lookalike. I need to up the intake of Marlboros and sidestep the side orders.

~

Someone's managed to walk out with half of the Rogues gallery. I'm quite flattered, but equally puzzled as to how they got past our security. At least they've left old George.

~

I've pretty much done all I can at Miss Q's. I need my old waistline and a new challenge. I'll just have the triple beef stack, skin-on fries and a couple of strawberry shakes for the road. You can't leave work on an empty stomach.

~

I'm catching up with my friend Magnus Fiennes, brother to Ralph and Joseph, a successful record producer/songwriter. He's with a Latin American beauty, who seems to be causing a bit of stir with our fellow drinkers. Apparently she is working with Magnus on her current world tour. I have, unquestionably, no face recognition skills whatsoever. I can talk to someone all night, pop to the loo for a pee, come back and reintroduce myself as if I've just met them. It's only when the waitress privately asks me how I know Shakira that I realise who it is.

~

An art tour with the wife. First stop Helsinki. I love this place. I feel like I've been brought up in captivity and just returned to my natural habitat. The city is army-barracks clean and index-orderly. They probably still have capital punishment here for litter louts.

~

We're wandering around Tuomiokirkko, a neoclassical, Lutheran cathedral that was completed in 1852. It's immaculate. I'm tempted to convert, then move here. It's a shame about the climate, though. In some parts of Finland winter lasts for as long as 200 days. I get

Seasonal Affective Disorder if I blink.

~

On to Saint Petersburg. My first and long-awaited trip to Russia. We're in the Hermitage Museum. Siobhan is hyperventilating. It's going to be a long day. I've overdosed on culture. I'm going to have to lie down. A fellow fatigued tourist has noticed my predicament.

'The things we do for our children, hey.'

'Erm… spouse.'

~

A party at Chocolate Towers, the London home of interior designer to the stars, Sera Loftus. She lives in the ultimate boho pad and tonight has hired a cool Latino band for everyone's entertainment. I've sat in on tambourine and shakers for the last few songs and the rhythm has seeped and shoehorned into my soul. I'm now one drink away from starting a mass conga and two drinks away from the Hokey Cokey.

~

Roger Taylor and Sarina Potgieter's wedding reception in the grounds of his rockstar pile in Surrey. Sarina has just kicked off proceedings with a fabulous flamenco display. Now, this is not your average wedding band on stage, with members of Queen, Pink Floyd, The Who, Pretenders and Def Leppard all performing. It's like a mini Live Aid, complete with a Bob Geldof rendition of The Waterboys classic, 'The Whole of the Moon'. Roger is that rare phenomenon (excluding the bloke in Paper Lace who sang 'Billy Don't Be a Hero'), a drummer with a great singing voice and finishes proceedings with a rousing rendition of David Bowie's 'Heroes', a song that takes me straight back to Checkpoint Charlie as if it was only yesterday.

~

The first London Lifestyle Awards. I'm on the judging panel. The nosh is not half-bad, the wine is flowing and I've just shared air space in the lift with the comic legend Leslie Phillips, so I can die peacefully now.

~

Caroline Citrin, who founded *Entertainment News* with me, has decided to strike out on her own and set up a new media agency. She has called it *The Media Eye* and has asked me to be a consultant one day a week. The timing is perfect, as my savings since leaving Miss Q's have taken quite a battering in the recent months I've spent as a gentleman of leisure, or 'between jobs', as I prefer to call it. The launch is tentatively set for February. We're meeting PR guru Matthew Freud this afternoon to see if there is any synergy with his company, Freud Communications.

~

Matthew was both helpful and encouraging, which has given Caroline the confidence boost to soldier on. We both know from our experience with *Entertainment News* that there's a shitload of hard graft ahead.

~

A quick coffee with my friend Tim Fenn to discuss the possibility of staging an Ibizan club awards event. His pitch is not really floating my boat. I'm all clubbed out and far more interested in his landscape garden business. My father once ran a garden nursery for a year or so on a break from the police force and I'd help out at weekends, so I guess a fertile seed was sown then, as I've since always been interested in all things horticultural. It's a complete contradiction with both my OCD and love of all things neon, but there you have it. Tim has suggested I work with him for a week and see if it grabs me.

~

It's the coldest winter on living record. Tim and I have just finished erecting a stack of fencing panels in a foot of snow. I've been up since 7 a.m., I can't feel my feet, my fingertips or my nose and the insides of my gloves have almost frozen solid. I've accidentally poured half a can of Ronseal into one of my wellies and clumsily taken a large chunk out of my ankle with a stray mallet and yet I'm having the time of my life.

~

The Full English breakfast has never tasted so good and the triple-strength builder's tea thawing out my fingers has given me a bigger boost than a Tijuana Toot. I've chucked in five sugars and I still can't taste any sweetness. I'm even getting a Masonic-like workman's nod from the nearby tables, an acknowledgment of my graft, being as it is that I am completely covered in mud from head to toe and my ears have turned Arctic blue.

~

A week in Northampton landscaping the grounds of a new yoga retreat. We're building a waterfall and just have to drain the ornamental pond. I'm draped in algae, up to my knees in freezing, foul-smelling and stagnant water. Tim's calling me.
    'Didn't you used to be Nick Valentine.'

~

Tim's lost his driving licence and he lives in Essex, so I've had to retire the secateurs. It's a terrible shame. I was just starting to notice muscles that I hadn't seen since my last trip to the Hall of Mirrors.

~

Robin Birley showed me around his new members' club in Shepherd Market today. It's still under construction, but it looks like it's going to be prodigious. Robin's last place, Annabel's in Berkeley Square, was founded by his father Mark Birley in 1963, who named it after his then wife Lady Annabel Vane-Tempest-Stewart. It has been *the* nightclub of choice for celebrities and society ever since.

~

A formal charity dinner hosted by Prince Charles at St James's Palace, with Sadie Frost and an old friend, John Joachim. I'm not quite sure what the event is in aid of exactly, as I'm a guest of John's, but it's quite nice to rough it every now and again.

~

Charles is making polite banter and nodding in all the right places with the assembled guests, who, one would imagine, he has zero interest in. I sure know how that feels.

~

I'm not a fan of black tie. James Bond pulls it off with great aplomb, whereas I always feel like I'm 11 years old again, a reluctant pageboy at my aunt's wedding, choking on tradition. Skid, on the other hand, says black tie is his favourite attire, as a cummerbund adds an inch to your height and takes three inches off your waistline.

~

Sad news. I've just read that the Hammersmith Palais, immortalised forever by The Clash, is to be demolished. This distinguished west London site, which first opened around 1919 as a ballroom dancing venue, is the reason I exist (with a little help from a winning sperm obviously), as my parents first locked eyes here in the early 50s at a jive contest. On that fateful evening, my mother walked off with second prize. My father walked off with my mother. Photos from that era show my old man in procession of a quiff so voluminous that it needed its own passport to travel. My mother, dare I say it, was quite a beauty and I can't help but notice that Tom looks incredibly smug in those faded snapshots, taken the night of their first encounter.

~

The Media Eye Christmas dinner at Inamo, a new oriental fusion restaurant in Soho that boasts a fully interactive ordering system built into your table. I can't get the hang of how it works. Every time I lean in to take a closer look, I inadvertently order another dish. My plate's overflowing and *The Media Eye* team are still waiting for their starters.

~

An invite to the launch of the London Sky Bar at Millbank Tower. I'm 29 floors up, knocking back complimentary cocktails while gazing out over panoramic views of my beloved metropolis. I just need a post-canapé ciggie. The problem is the smoking area is on the ground floor. By the time I've made it back to the bar, I'm ready for another fag.

~

Siobhan and I are leading very separate lives. I guess the considerable age gap is the main reason… though on some rare days I *don't* feel younger than her 27 years.

~

The Box nightclub has opened in London. I'm here with the DJ Rubber Ron, a much-loved father figure in the fetish world who started Club Submission in 1989 and was one of the main liberating lights to take the scene into the mainstream. The transsexual on stage had just removed a bottle from his/her arse and sprayed the baying front tables as a grand finale. Ron and I both agree that's quite a hard act to follow.

~

Drinks at Whisky Mist in Mayfair with Nick House. Nick seems to open a new venue in London every other week. People often confuse us and I constantly receive texts asking me for launch invites to nightspots that I don't even know exist. One positive aspect of this is that, if I am pulled up on any mild misdemeanour, I tell them they are probably mixing me up with Nick House.

~

The Media Eye launched today. Caroline reckons she's aged a decade in the last four months. My input has been fairly minimal this time around, so I feel for her. The product is great though. She just needs people to switch over from our old baby, *Entertainment News*.

~

I've run into my friend Rosalind Milani Gallieni. She is in a panic. Ros owns a PR company specialising in luxury goods and is supposed to deliver a House of Worth couture dress to Paris in the morning. Unfortunately, her staff member tasked with the chore has been taken sick.

'I don't suppose you fancy a trip to Paris, do you?'

'Why not.'

~

It's my first trip on Eurostar. A decisively stress-free way for me to travel with my fear of flying. It's also quite satisfying to be returning to Paris sober. The dress is worth a small fortune, so it is a great relief to offload it.

~

I'm being a right old tourist. I've even lunched on the obligatory tough-as-old-boots steak and chips at a restaurant far too close to the French capital's main station for comfort. It's a beautiful sunny day, so a river cruise down the Seine seems as good a way as any to while away my time.

~

I've overturned the dreadful steak I suffered earlier with an al fresco, snapping fresh, lobster salad dinner and a bottle of France's finest. I think being a courier could be my calling.

~

U'Luvka Vodka has taken me on as an ambassador on the recommendation of Tara Viesnik, who used to work with me at Cuckoo. I can only assume that the offer has come on the back of a blind tasting I once did with her, where I declared it to be my favourite vodka. There's definitely worse jobs to be had. I wonder if they need anything delivered. Skid says it's like putting a paedophile in charge of Hamleys.

~

Drinks and dinner at Eric Yu's Salvador & Amanda tapas restaurant and bar in Covent Garden with my mate, DJ and Wag Club founder, Chris Sullivan, and his fellow spinner Spencer Mac, who seems to always be behind the decks at every new club or cool party I swing into. It turns out Spencer and I live in the same street in west London. I suggest we get a 'St Margarets Till I Die' tattoo, but he's not convinced.

~

Prince William and Kate Middleton get married today. Colin and I are toasting the newlyweds with a right royal rattle up on the Kings Road in Chelsea. No one likes a killjoy.

~

A shimmering sunset over Cap d'Antibes. U'Luvka Vodka is supplying stock for a Maybach Foundation charity dinner, organised by Juno Productions, at the Imperial Garoupe Hotel with Quincy Jones and Kanye West as guests of honour. I've landed right on my sun-kissed feet with this one.

~

Aloe Blacc is performing an emotive, acoustic set in beautiful surroundings. I've had to introduce myself to Quincy, just so as to touch the hand of genius. He looks pretty friggin' good for 78, having outlived many of the stars whose careers he audibly shaped. I now have an OCD dilemma. Wash the hand? Don't wash the hand?

~

The nature of what I do is by its very nature all or nothing. I can be living the high life in exulted company one moment, twiddling my thumbs, pondering my next project and pay cheque the next. It would probably be a lot more stressful if I knew any different. I don't.

~

Another consultancy offer. This time it's for a new bistro/bar/ boutique hotel in Ladbroke Grove, to be called Portobello House. It's on the site of the old Earl Percy pub. I love working on projects that are more than just money-spinners for the owners and this is certainly the case with Guy and Lara. There's not a whole lot I can add to what they have already meticulously achieved, but I am starting off by compiling their music playlists for the bistro, a job I love doing. Track 1. CD 1. We'll kick off with a bit of Maria Callas, I think.

~

A call from Koe Naiche, a six foot seven, half-Welsh, half-Native American, singer/songwriter who I first saw perform at Miss Q's. He wants to know if I would be interested in helping his band Tribal Law secure a record deal. I've said I'm happy to take him out on the London lap and he can schmooze while I booze. He is a formidable presence, deeply immersed in Native American culture and a pretty unrivalled guitarist at that.

~

The Playboy Club has returned to London after a 30-year or so absence. As Koe and I walk the red carpet we are heckled by a group of women protesting about the sexual objectification of women. We certainly look an odd couple. Me in specs and a pinstripe suit, him in full warrior regalia. Hugh Heffner doesn't seem particularly bothered by this demonstration taking place outside, settled as he is on his throne, surrounded by busty bunnies.

~

Jamie Lorenz has asked me to come back to The Cuckoo Club as creative director. Barbara Hulanicki, who founded the iconic Biba fashion label in 1964 and set the style for the decade to follow, has been signed up to redesign Cuckoo's interior. All clubs, no matter how successful, need a major facelift every few years to keep the dough-dropping denizens coming back for more and this is quite a coup on Jamie's part.

~

Back in the old office. It feels like I never left. Gordon Martin, Cuckoo's Dionysian table manager, is especially welcoming, as he figures the blame for any twilight wrongdoings can now be split equally between the two of us.

~

Jamie's cousin David now seems to be running the organisation of promoters, DJs and table spenders. He is 24. I'm really starting to feel my age.

~

I'm often asked what I actually do for a living and I answer truthfully that I'm still trying to work that out, 33 years after I first started working.

~

A meeting in the Cuckoo office with my friend Jemma Kidd to discuss the launch party at Cuckoo for her new line of cosmetics. Unfortunately, Jamie has got to my desk before me and completely covered it, along with my chair, computer, phone and drawers, in more than a thousand or so Post-it Notes.

~

Jamie is an unrelenting practical joker. Last week, he played a trick on me where we arm-wrestled and then he withdrew his hand suddenly and nearly knocked my front teeth out. I repaid Jamie by signing him up to a load of S&M dating sites on his work email address, an eye-opening education for *me* in itself.

~

The Keep a Child Alive Black Ball at the Roundhouse. The Cuckoo Club is running the cocktail bar. Tonight's guest performers include Alicia Keys, who is hosting the event, Mark Ronson and Paloma Faith. One of Cuckoo's top mixologists, Gavin Forbes, has just created a bespoke cocktail for indie rock band Gossip's Beth Ditto at her table, which has given me an idea. I've asked him to create a cool drink especially for me, a hard task as my usual tipple these days is Delboy's favourite, the Pina Colada.

~

Every time I return to the counter to retrieve my drink after a fag break, the bar staff start laughing. Whatever is causing them such merriment is utterly lost on me. Gavin is practically wetting himself.

'Ok, tell me.'

'I've loaded your drink up with straws, fruit, garnish, crushed ice and the bloody kitchen sink, every time you go out, until your glass is about three foot high and you haven't even noticed.'

~

Colin used to do a similar thing when I stayed with him, if we ever hit his local Asda for a communal shop. I'd get to the counter and the checkout girl would avert her gaze as she quickly scanned the tube of haemorrhoid cream, vaginal wipes and adolescent spot wash that Colin had just slipped surreptitiously into my basket.

~

I'm settled in the bar of Knightsbridge's Beauchamp Club, while American author Jay McInerney reads from his 1984 epic novel *Bright Lights, Big City*, a depiction of cocaine culture. It all sounds strangely familiar. Way too familiar.

~

My mobile hasn't stopped ringing all morning. *The Mail Online* has run a story saying I once stepped out with Keira Knightley (I don't think so) and is now linking me with Russian supermodel Natalia Vodianova (we've never even met). Apparently, Natalia and I have hired a nice little cottage together where we are relaxing and partying. Now I've suffered from memory loss in the past, but I would definitely, definitely, definitely remember that.

~

A succulent mooing steak at the launch of the revered Austrian chef Wolfgang Puck's Cut restaurant at 45 Park Lane, courtesy of the hotel group's charming PR girl. It's Wolfgang's first venture in Europe, having come to prominence at the two-Michelin-starred Spago Beverly Hills. He's also the official caterer for the Oscars.

~

Now I love fine dining, but I'm also equally at home in my local burger joint. My first-ever job was actually as a dishwasher at the Teddington Wimpy, aged about 13. Boy, were those dishes clean.

~

Siobhan and I have separated, but remain the best of friends. It's been an utterly amiable split and she's shipped off to Shoreditch (which is a tad more happening than good old St Margarets). In fact, we probably get on better now than when we were together.

~

Skid thinks *The Mail Online* story is hilarious and keeps asking me how things are going with Natalia, while Siobhan's sent me a barrage of emails with links to cottages to rent.

~

Thierry Guetta, aka Mr Brainwash, is having dinner at the Cuckoo. Mr. Brainwash shot to fame as the subject of urban artist Banksy's documentary *Exit Through the Gift Shop*, a comical exposé of the art world. It's great to see the hype and spirit of Andy Warhol getting another outing, with the same financial consequences.

~

Caprice, the American-born model, is at Cuckoo today, auditioning lingerie models for a fashion show at her forthcoming birthday party. Unfortunately for her, the DJ hasn't turned up so I've had to step into the breach and spin a few tunes while her hotties shake their stuff on the dance floor… and she's thanking me.

~

It's Skid's birthday so we're tucking into pizza and Otis tunes at Ciro Orsini's Pizza Pomodoro in Knightsbridge. I always keep an eye on Skid's hairline, figuring as he's eight years older than me, as soon as he starts thinning, I'm on an eight-year countdown to the combover. So far, so good.

~

To Monaco with Marcus Molina, The Cuckoo Club's VIP host, for MICS, the Monaco International Clubbing Show. This annual event aims to bring all the key players from the worldwide nightlife industry into one area, namely the Grimaldi Forum. For me, it's a great excuse to check out the Egyptian thread-count at the Monte Carlo Bay Hotel.

~

A fine thread-count indeed. It's just a shame I didn't get to experience it. After the exhibition I ran into Jonathan Martinelli, an old friend who was on a night off from his close protection work for a European property magnate, and we ended up painting the town rouge. I've made it back to the hotel in time for check-out, though curiously I'm covered in feathers and popcorn.

~

I'm Siobhan's, or the ex-wife as I'm now addressing her, plus-one for the British Fashion Awards at the Savoy Theatre. The ex-wife works part-time for Manolo Blahnik. When she first moved in with me, we had to hire a man with a van just to transport her shoe collection to its new home. I had to triple my contents insurance and that was just for the everyday wear ones.

~

The paps have gone into a frenzy, so I guess Victoria Beckham has arrived, or maybe it's Kate Hudson or Samantha Cameron or Georgia May Jagger, all of who are attending tonight. Siobhan's on a high, but it's all a bit too air/arse kissy for me. I think Cuckoo's calling.

~

I'm in desperate need of sun, sea and sand and Samoa is certainly not lacking in any of the tropical trinity. The plane journey was absolute purgatory and it feels like I left London about a week ago. Actually, it's so far I probably did. Still, I have three whole weeks before I have to suffer the journey home. I just hope I can get some more Valium, as I'd popped most of my supply before I had even touched down in Dubai, the first leg of the journey.

~

What a beautiful place. It's incredibly lush and seemingly unspoilt. Peculiarly, every second building appears to be a church, a hand-down from the island's missionary past, I guess. Samoa is actually split into two islands: Upolu, where I'm staying, and Savai'i. I've already gone native, having slipped into a lava-lava, a traditional type of sarong.

~

You could not get any further away from clubland than Samoa, which is the whole point of this trip. There are surprisingly few tourists. I'm staying in a traditional hut right on the beach and I haven't seen another European for days. It's bliss. The perfect place to continue working on my life story.

~

It's not surprising how writing about the past stirs up buried emotions. I had a right old sob today when I started recalling my mother's death. These were the first tears shed since her funeral 30-odd years ago. I also cried a few tears, but strictly of the laughing variety, thinking about the time my father, towards the end of his life, went for a trim in his local salon and thought he had charmed and pulled the 'smoking hot hairdresser' when she only charged him half the advertised price, only to then notice a sign offering OAPs 50% discount on submission of proof of age.

'I wouldn't have minded but she didn't even ask for my ID.'

~

I've bid Samoa a very fond farewell. I feel completely recharged and I'm very much looking forward to catching up with Richard, aka Tarzan from *Brothers*, who lives on the south island of New Zealand in Christchurch. I don't think anything could break the Zen-like state I've sunk into over the last week or so… with perhaps the exception of an earthquake.

~

The first quake measured 5.8 on the Richter scale, the second, 6.0, followed by a score of aftershocks. It's fucking terrifying when you are not used to it, unlike the poor locals who have suffered incredibly destructive summer and winter quakes this year alone.

'Welcome to Christchurch, mate.'

~

A shuddering aftershock.

~

Another aftershock.

~

And yet another thunderous tremble. I know they are only echoes of the first quake, but my nerves are shot to pieces. I keep thinking the next quake is going to be the pessimistically predicted big one that completely wipes out the city.

~

This must be the only time in my life that I've genuinely looked forward to getting on a plane. Admittedly, it's just the lesser of two evils.

~

We're on our final descent. Heathrow Airport has never looked so enticing. I can't wait to kiss the tarmac. Home sweet bloody home.

~

A preview screening of *One More: A Definitive History of UK Clubbing 1988–2008* with a few of the definitive DJs, namely Danny Rampling, Tall Paul, Brandon Block and Nicky Holloway, in attendance. I haven't seen Nicky since 1988, the whole period the documentary covers.

'As I was saying…'

~

Watching *One More* makes me realise just how much I've missed. I've paradoxically travelled to well over 40 different countries, but barely scraped the surface of the British Isles in my pursuit of pills and thrills. Mind you, this is the cool side of clubbing, whereas I've been more involved in what Colin would describe as the 'wankier' end of the industry.

~

It's Valentine's night. I'm at a party at a friend's house. I've drunk way too much and really should leave, though have just started an animated conversation with one of the female guests about my time in Los Angeles.

~

'You didn't?'
    'I did.'
    'No, surely not.'
    'Surely.'

'You fucking idiot.'

Skid cannot believe my stupidity. At 4 a.m. I thought it would be a good idea to book morning flights to LA for myself and my drinking companion. I must have then passed out. The tickets are non-refundable because of the time scale, so I wasted the best part of a grand on a pissed-up whim. When I called the girl just now to fill in the blanks, she told me that I should think myself lucky as she wanted to fly first class, but only economy was available. The funny thing is I can never remember the security password on my credit card when I'm *sober*.

~

Dinner at the recently opened Novikov restaurant and bar with Jori White, who does their PR. I first met Jori in the mid-90s and have dined somewhat lavishly at her expense (account) ever since. That said, I have always plugged her latest venue and recommended her services to any new place that needs a great PR. The latest being Dabbous, set up by former Cuckoo Club employees Ollie Dabbous and Oscar Kinberg and destined for culinary distinction.

~

A club trawl. I'm starting at The Arts Club in Dover Street, where Dale Davis is playing with the house band tonight. The original club was opened in 1863 but has recently undergone a major refurb and relaunch, where Gwyneth Paltrow joined Dale on stage for a rendition of Cee Lo Green's 'Forget/Fuck You' in front of guest of honour and club patron, Prince Philip.

~

On to Rose to see Mikkel Kongerslev, my old bar manager at Molton House by way of Aura, Project and Luxx, where former Cuckoo bar manager Andreas Jansson works his magic and, finally, Cirque du Soir on the home straight. This is the thing with London clubland, it's incredibly incestuous. It's hard to enter any venue without chancing upon someone you have worked with in the past.

Sometimes for the bad, sometimes for the better.

~

Andreas and I once had a close scrape after a party in Cannes, when a local taxi driver tried to rip us off. Andreas and the guy squared up and I misguidedly jumped between them, just as the driver produced a rather unsavoury-looking blade, which Andreas tried to kick out of his hand but instead floored me with a perfect roundhouse. Luckily the irate knife-wielder then thought better of it and shot off into the darkness unscathed, whereas my tender ribs ached all the way back to London.

~

It's London society boy Alex Maclean's birthday party at the revamped Scotch of St James club. This intimate venue, tucked down an innocuous alleyway, was the place where Jimi Hendrix played his first London gig way back in 1966. I'm taking it easy tonight as I once woke up in a wardrobe at Blakes Hotel at one of Alex's previous celebrations.

'I wondered where you had got to. What's with the hanger in the back of your jacket?'

~

Henry Lytton-Cobbold is a big fan of Miles Winter Roberts, so has asked Miles and me to perform at his 50th birthday party at his home, Knebworth House. This estate has staged some of the biggest concerts in the history of rock, so I am taking great delight in telling people that I am playing Knebworth. I'm just failing to mention that it's in the grand hall, not the grounds, and that it's to 150 or so people, not the usual 125,000.

~

I've switched from bongos to cajon, a Peruvian drum that you sit on to play. It arrived in the post yesterday. The gig's tonight.

~

Henry's just made a birthday speech in his birthday suit, with nothing but a red bowler hat to cover his modesty. We're away. On the first hit of the first bar of the first song, I whack myself in the goolies. I've given suffering for your art a whole new meaning. I just need to make it to the end of the song and grab a quick breather.

~

The pain has finally subsided in time for the encore.
    'Thank you. Goodnight.'

~

Back to Cannes for the film festival as a guest of Belvedere Vodka. Every year they take a group of London club bods on a two-day drinking marathon. Tonight is the main event, a party at the VIP Room at the JW Marriott Hotel. Eighties songstress Cyndi Lauper is banging out her hits and has just been joined onstage by Ronnie Wood, not an altogether obvious collaboration. I'm going to call it a night and head back to the Hotel de Mougins so that I can get up early tomorrow and catch some rays.

~

Rain.

~

Another big night last night at Gotha. I'm glad it's only a short flight back to London as I am feeling decidedly edgy today.

~

'Cabin crew to your seats immediately.'
    The words I dread to hear, then suddenly...

We've just fallen out of the sky like a lead balloon dropped into a spin dryer. Suffice to say the cabin crew have not made it to their seats. They appear to be plastered to the roof of the plane. My arms and legs are shaking uncontrollably. The woman in the seat in front of me is crying hysterically.

'We're going to die. We're going to die.'

She is totally inconsolable. I'm holding hands with the girl in the seat next to me. We have not said a word to each other up to this point. The guy next to her has peed himself. I've just clocked Eddie, Cuckoo's bar manager, who told me just before take-off that he actually enjoys a bit of turbulence. He is as white as a sheet. My palms are sweating. My stomach's curdling. I'm having to force myself to breathe. Another massive shudder. More screams from behind me.

'Oh my God, oh my God, oh my God.'

I'm utterly convinced we are going to crash. Random thoughts from my past flash into my brain. My first family holiday, my last day at school. I'm imagining the headlines, assuming that clubland is going to be missing a hell of a lot of people in the next few minutes. A final whispered request to my guardian angel.

'Stick the kettle on, Mum, I'll be with you shortly.'

Then it's all over as abruptly as it started. The plane has steadied itself. There's absolute silence along the whole length of the aisle, bar a few scattered whimpers. It feels like the collective shock onboard has frozen us in time. I'm in a zombie-like trance for the final 20 minutes of the journey, waiting for my heart's BPM to drop a few decimal points. We land to a hugely relieved chorus of celebratory cheers. The pilot has coyly come out of the cockpit. He looks pretty shaken up too. He tells me it's his worst experience in 30 years of flying. I tell him it's my worst experience in 49 years of living.

~

Duran Duran's management are throwing Nick Rhodes a secret 50th birthday party and have asked me to help organise it. I've found a fantastic venue, One Mayfair, a Grade-1 listed building built in 1825 in the Greek revival style, which was formerly St

Mark's Church. The evening will kick off with a cocktail reception at Hamiltons Gallery, where more than 200 artworks will be displayed, created by Nick's friends and family around the theme 'The Devil and Nick Rhodes'.

~

Everyone is leaving the gallery and heading to the church. I've pulled a favour with my friend Amanda Davis from AD Design and she has decked out One Mayfair in spectacular style. The security guys are not quite ready when the first guest arrives and have told him to come back in ten minutes. Unfortunately, it's Ricky Gervais so I'm chasing down the road, like a crazed fan, trying to catch him and explain that he can indeed enter now. As his car pulls away, I turn to my left and notice a full restaurant of people observing my undignified dash.

~

Ricky's come back to the party, oblivious to my Usain Bolt impression. He's keen to know how much this surprise cost to put on. I would guess about double the initial budget at this stage, though I have to say Nick looks pretty chuffed, as do the rest of the band who paid for tonight. Dom Brown, who has spent the last seven years as the guitarist with Duran, has even suggested he launch his solo album *Brown to Blue* at Cuckoo next week.

~

Dom's band tonight features his father Rob and floating members of Groove Armada and Faithless. I've also worked my way onto the stage, by way of a cameo appearance on congas and even managed not to tap the wedding tackle this time.

~

The annual staple catch-up that is… The London Club and Bar Awards 2012. I swear there are quite a few people here that I only ever see at this event. Tommy Mack, party promoter and merry maniac, is one of them. He's a walking, talking tornado and we've all been put on hurricane alert. Tonight I've nabbed the Up All Night Award (shared with half of London). A fellow guest congratulates me and asks exactly what the award is for. I jokingly tell him that it honours heavy drug consumption and then ask what club he works for.

'I don't. I'm a journalist for the BBC.'

~

A concert in Hyde Park featuring Duran Duran, Sterophonics, Snow Patrol and Paolo Nutini to celebrate the start of the London Olympics. The Red Arrows have just performed a spectacular fly-by, trailing the colours of the Union Jack. I feel atypically patriotic and the atmosphere is electric. We are hosting the official Duran Duran after-party at Cuckoo, so I have to take my leave and check everything is in order back at the club.

~

There seems to be a collective Olympic fever permeating the party. I was worried, after a lot of despondent talk, that guests would not be able to make their way to the club because of the West End being gridlocked but my fears are totally unfounded as Piccadilly is totally clear, so I guess the scaremongering has worked in our favour.

~

I'm off to Mykonos with my new love Katherine to review a few hotels for the revamped *Epicurean Life* magazine, including the critically acclaimed Kivotos. This sumptuous sanctuary, overlooking Ornos Bay, features its own private beach and a selection of 42 tastefully designed rooms and suites, including Noah's Villa with its luxurious penthouse and a bedroom that you can literally swim into. The hotel also provides its own 25-metre private yacht, captain and crew should the urge to pop to another bay take you.

~

Across the island to Panormos Beach to meet Sarina and Roger Taylor and Scottish, sanguine fashion designer Julien Macdonald for lunch. Roger, despite being in the third-biggest selling band of all time behind the Beatles and Led Zeppelin, is a very unassuming bloke and his presence is almost unnoticed until the restaurant owner takes it upon himself to put on 'We are the Champions' at a deafening volume, halfway through dessert. Roger takes it with great humour, even posing for a few photos for the restaurant staff, before slowly slipping beneath his baseball cap.

~

Julien had a fashion week party at Cuckoo not long after we first opened and was flour-bombed as he arrived, arm in arm with Paris Hilton, by fur protestors from Peta, the animal rights campaigners. He took it all in his mini, mischievous stride, dusted himself off and partied with guest DJ Pete Tong into the night. A shrinking violet he is not. The flour residue that settled on a few of the club's tables led more than a few late arrivals to think a Colombian Christmas had arrived early.

~

'I can't believe it's all ending this year, mate.'
    'What, the Mayan prophecy?'
    'No, me turning 50,' I tell Skid.

~

My 50th birthday party at Cuckoo. It's a swan song as much as a celebration, as I will pretty much be leaving the club after tonight to concentrate on finishing my book.

~

It's great to see so many friends, old and new, particularly David Cuff who I first befriended at infant school in 1966 and shared practically every adolescent high and low with for the first 16 years of my life. It's hard to believe I'm one year off the age of my mother when she died. She would have loved tonight, as would my father Tom. My sister Jane is stuck in the highlands, so Skid is drinking for both of them. The theme for tonight's bash is 'Fuck Me, I'm 50' and that's exactly how I feel. I can't comprehend I've already had half a century. Damn, did that fly by!

~

It feels like only yesterday that I was at the Walton Hop, my first tentative tiptoe into nocturnal naughtiness, when nightclubs were still called discos. I can still remember that sick feeling in my stomach as I plucked up the courage to ask a skinny blonde girl with large jugs (as boobs were colloquially known as in the mid-70s) for a slow dance to the backdrop of Rose Royce's smooching classic, 'Wishing on a Star'.

'What's this, charity night? Piss off.'

~

David Cuff and I are reminiscing. He turned 50 in March. His father Bob, who died in 2010, was like a second father to me while growing up and was quite a famous matte artist, working on many feature films, including *The Guns of Navarone*, *Dr Strangelove* and *The Life of Brian*. Bob was also once comically commissioned to render Jayne Mansfield's bust more respectable for a TV show in the 50s.

~

David himself works in television and is currently in the process of bidding for his own channel. I remind him of our underage trips to the Nashville pub in West Kensington aged 16, where he had to get the drinks in while I hid behind a pillar, looking about 14 years old as I did. I was still regularly asked for ID right into my early 20s, which was a great source of embarrassment, particularly when on a first date.

~

It's funny, the ageing process. Everything on the inside stays 18, then you look in the mirror one day and it's your grandfather staring back at you, Dorian Gray style.

~

Back to Spencer Mac's to continue the celebration.

~

It's 11 a.m. At this rate I won't make 51, least of all another half a century.

~

A stiffy in the post. An invite to Diego Bivero-Volpe and Antoin Commane's new Austrian alpine restaurant, bar and disco, Bodo's Schloss. I feel like I need to lie down in a very dark room for at least a week before I can contemplate going out again.

~

Detox done. Time for some retox. I've dropped by Cuckoo to pick up my birthday presents, which I sensibly left behind after my party. Will.i.am has called in for a quick drink. I'm going to miss this place.

~

A call from my friend Mark Hladnik. He is opening a new restaurant/club in Fulham called Barbarella. Will I co-host the opening party with PR/party boy Jack Freud?

~

The launch has gone well, though I broke two toes yesterday accidentally kicking my dining room table while running to answer the phone. It was a wrong number. Gary Lineker's wife ran over his foot on their way here tonight, so we're both hobbling around Barbarella… the walking wounded.

~

My friend James has turned up with *American Pie* actress Tara Reid, who is staying with him at the moment. The party is in its final throes, so we've decided to all head back to his house.

~

It's 5 a.m. and time to call it a night/morning. The trouble is, I've let myself out and now can't find the release button for the 12-foot high security gates. It's raining cats, I don't know which bell James is and he's not answering his phone.

~

James has finally picked up my call. It's 6 a.m. I look like a drowned rat dipped in an ice bucket and hung on a meat hook.

~

Never in my life has a hot shower felt so good. The security release button was right in front of me all along. Time for a trip to Specsavers.

~

Colin's 50th birthday dinner at Rock and Rose in Kew. He's managed what I always dreamed of doing, namely retiring at 50. He has jacked in his job, pimped up his three-bedroom flat and plans to advertise it as a holiday let so he can spend the rest of his life travelling, partying and pottering.

'Welcome to my world, Colin.'

~

I'm helping the guys from Hus Gallery put on a solo show at One Marylebone for Welsh artist Mark Evans. It's entitled Furious Affection and is part of Frieze Art week. Mark produces his sociopolitical pieces by carving intricate images out of animal hides. They are incredible. I suggested we hire a bucking bronco to sit outside the venue to draw the attention of people passing by, but we've ended up with two live cows painted pink and green respectively. Cue the acid flashback.

~

There's a mixed bag of celebs in attendance tonight. As well as Mark, we have Julian Lennon, Chris Eubank and Grandmaster Flash, who I met recently at Cuckoo. I struggled that night over how to introduce him to people. Grand? Grandmaster? Flash? His birth name is actually Joseph and a nicer guy you could not expect to meet. As well as being a hip hop pioneer, he is also attributed as inventing the crossfader, an instrument that I've never quite mastered.

~

It had to happen. I've finally succumbed to *The X Factor*. Just watched Ella Henderson tear a new arse in Minnie Ripperton's 'Loving You.' An astonishing version of a near-perfect classic. The panel seemed genuinely stunned. It's now down to the great British public. Good luck with that one.

~

Ella aside, it's fairly depressing how throwaway the music industry has become these days. When I was in my late teens, the bands you followed defined your life, not recorded your ringtone.

~

Dinner at Hampton Court House with Skid and Katherine. We're the guests of Julian Stewart Lindsay, who occasionally teaches music here as it's a private school by day. It's hearty fayre and live jazz so I'm in my element. Julian has suggested that Skid and I jam with the pianist, so my brother's popped out his harmonica and I'm improvising with some brushes and a single snare drum. It's the first time Skid and I have ever played together. I'm faking it with the 5/4 and just about managing to pull it off. Skid, on the other hand, has received a seated ovation as he solos on 'Summertime'.

~

As a Londoner, budget permitting, you could eat out 365 times a year, at a different restaurant every day, without repeating yourself. Admittedly, you'd probably have coronary failure before you completed the task, but the choice on offer here is overwhelming nevertheless.

~

Tonight, it's Coya, a new modern Peruvian restaurant/bar in Piccadilly, which I briefly consulted on for LA Entertainment's Ariel Vadee and Luis Villamizar in an early incarnation. The place looks paradisiacal and the food is truly exquisite. It's hard to believe just a year ago I was showing people around a huge empty shell and then spending the rest of the evening blowing cement dust out of my party holes.

~

A vocal warm-up exercise in the taxi before hitting B Soho pizzeria for a few rounds of karaoke. Colin is the perfect singing partner, being as he is in possession of a brilliant voice. The trick while duetting with him is to show all the emotion of the song, but actually mime, then humbly accept all the ensuing accolades. The only problem is if Colin for whatever reason stops emoting mid-song, as he does tonight, you're fucked.

~

I'm off for a coffee at The Society Club, a café/bar/art gallery and bookshop in Soho with Robert Pereno, who first appeared on the London club scene in the early 80s, fronting the New Romantic band Shock, and never left. He wants me to meet publisher-turned-agent Carrie Kania, who now works at Conville & Walsh, as he thinks she could help with my book.

~

The meeting with Carrie went extremely well. We bonded over Warholian tales and our shared love of T. Rex. I've left her with a synopsis of my book and 60 sample pages, so now it's in the lap of the gods.

~

Back to The Society Club for a talk to be given by Leee Black Childers, who is promoting his new book, *Drag Queens, Rent Boys, Rockstars and Punks*. Lee was a deep-rooted part of Warhol's Factory entourage and so was well placed to photographically document the nihilistic rock/art scene of the late 60s and 70s. His playground was clubs like CBGB's, Max's Kansas City and Studio 54, and his images reflect a scene that was too fast to live, too young to die and too strung out to wonder why. Tonight's Q&A is informative, funny and touching. By all accounts, having lived the life he has, Leee shouldn't be here to tell the story.

~

A resounding positive response from Carrie. I now have an agent.

~

And a publisher. Carrie sent my book package to a new online publishing house called Unbound and they've signed me on the spot.

~

I've cleared TK Maxx out of tweed and moleskin: a dress rehearsal for a new vocation. Author! A solitary profession for serious souls, troubled with the daily consideration of life's unanswered conundrums and the search for the point of the pontificator... But, then again.

~

A celebration dinner at Distrkt nightclub with Skid and Colin. The food is surprisingly good for club grub. We skip the After Eights and instead opt for the Up To Eights, which in turn leads to a very long discussion about the title of my book. As dawn breaks, I nail it. It was right under my nose. I've just got to write another 42,000 words and try and remember the last 35 years of revelry... Now, how did it all start?

Acknowledgements

An enormous thanks to:
Carrie Kania at Conville & Walsh – my guiding literary light.

Extra special thanks to:

Ameen Rawat
Caroline Citrin
Colin Hilton
Jonathan Martinelli
Julian Stewart Lindsay
Katherine Wee
Kevin Carvill
Mark Armstrong
Mark Duvauchelle
Mark Sloper
Nick Rhodes
Roger Taylor
Sarina Taylor
Siobhan O'Hagan
Spencer Mac
Unbound

Special thanks to:
Akashia Hoosein-Carswell
Alexis MacDonald
Alice Temperley
Andrew Loveday
Andy Hobsbawm
Andy Warhol
Asi O'Hagan
Ayman Alghafar
Azzy Asghar
Babette Kulik

Bobby Lorenz
Bruce MacDonald
Chris Hufford
Chris Sullivan
Danny Dyer
David Cuff
David Driver
David Eastman
David Gosling
Eamonn Wilmott
Emma Birtwhistle
Eric Corsaletti-Delgado
Estelle MacDonald
Fan Costi
Fin Wild
Grandmaster Flash
Guy Chambers
Hannah Wright
Hannibal Reitano
Henry Cobbold
Hilary Fairhirst
Hugh Cornwell
Jake Panayioto
James Fierro
Jamie Bloom
Jamie Lorenz
Jason Gale
Jonathan Rich

Jori White
Julian Clary
Julian Dunkerton
Katharine Walsh
Katie Maloy
Katy Krassner
Kevin Witt
Mandy Miami
Mark Fuller
Mark Hix
Mark Pritchard
Martin Dunkerton
Meg Mathews
Michelle Carvill
Nathan Coombs
Nicky Haslam
Nicky Holloway

Paul Moran
Piers Hernu
Rachel Rigby Jones
Rebecca Claydon
Richard Young
Robert Pereno
Robin Duff
Rusty Egan
Simon Mills
Steve Currie
Steve Tabakin
Stevie Wilde
Tara Palmer Tomkinson
Tom Parker Bowles
Tom Poole
Wendy Laister

Apologies to anyone that I may have failed to include.
My memory is not quite what it used to be.

Subscribers

Unbound is a new kind of publishing house. Our books are funded directly by readers. This was a very popular idea during the late 18th and early 19th centuries. Now we have revived it for the internet age. It allows authors to write the books they really want to write and readers to support the writing they would most like to see published.

The names listed below are of readers who have pledged their support and made this book happen. If you'd like to join them, visit: www.unbound.co.uk.

Vangelis Alexiou
Ayman Alghafar
Hannibal Martin Anchorena
    Reitano
Mark Armstrong
Azzy Asghar
Andy Ash
Jasmin Athwal
Monica Axelsson
Robert Batchelor
Matthew Benson
Alec Bentley
Clayton Berger
Emma Birtwistle
Georgie Black
Edward Bloom
Jamie Bloom
Natasha Bloom
Ad Bradley
Liz Brewer

Tim Bromfield
Dom Brown
Colin Butts
Sarah Canet
Yvette Carter
Kevin Carvill
Melanie Catchpole
Gregory Cathcart
Peter Cattaneo
Laurie Cesek
Stefano Cestra
Lee Chapman
Paul Charlton
Charlie Chauhan
Serena Chee
Tav Christopher
Caroline Citrin
Julia Clancey
Rebecca Claydon
Henry Cobbold

Don Cochrane
Nat Coombsn
Chris Cooper
Eric Corsaletti-Delgado
Fan Costi
John Crawford
David Cuff
Cuff Media
Deborah Curtiss
Antonello Dato
Ivan Davies
Amanda Davis
Dale Davis
Patrick Deane
Gina Decio
Elizabeth Deegan
Kate Denston
Eric de Rothschild
Alicia de la Torre
Alexandra Dixon
Miggy Drummond
Martin Dunkerton
Marc Julius Duvauchelle
James Ebdon
Knut Eikrem
Clio Elliott
Rod Elliott
Eleanor Evans
Hilary Fairhurst
Oliver FairhurstOliverF
Cai Ferrer
James Fierro
Gavin Forbes
John Fossey
Ilana Fox
Isobel Frankish
Alastair Gallichan
Rosalind Gallieni

Rock Galpin
John Garrett
Will Geddes
Skaiste Giedraityte-Gilbert
Clare Gillespie
Henrietta Goddard
William Gordon-Martin
David Gosling
Angela Gosnell
Brett Gregory-Peake
Zoe Griffin
Richard Grindy
Peter Hadfield
Piers Harris
Jeremy Hartley
Caitlin Harvey
Piers Hernu
Claire Higgins
Mark Hiley
Richard J Hills
Colin Hilton
Emily Hilton
Lucinda Ella Hilton
Oscar Hilton
Andy Hobsbawm
Gillian Hoffman
Zoë Holbrook
Akashia Hoosein Carswell
Frank Horovitch
Alex Houstoun-Boswall
Ruth Howlett
Chris Hufford
Saxon Jackson
Emma Jacob
Andreas Jansson
Strawberry Jefferson
Soren Jessen
Donagh Kane

Nathan Kay
Ruben Kazumian
Peter Kellet
Charlotte Kelly
Eddie Krasniqi
Ignacy Kundzicz
Marc Lapeyre
Nina Lauc
Jim Lawton
Alexandra Lewis-Wortley
Lena Lieder
Lin Lin
Teddy Lindsay
Tony Linkin
JM Littman
Finlay Logan
David Lorenz
James Lorenz
Robert Lorenz
Andrew Loveday
Theo Lovett
Khaled Lowe
M M
John Mc Donnell
Craig McCall
Spencer Mccallum
Alex Maclean
Katie Maloy
Adam Marshall
Dan Marshall
Jonathan Martinelli
James Melvin
Lauren Mezzina
Peter Milburn
Remy Millar
John Mitchinson
Susie Moore
Faraz Nagree

Koe Naiche
Richard Nolan
Mikael Noyan
Catherine Nunn
Siobhan O'Hagan
James Orr
David Osmon
Tom Patrouille
Julius Peploe
Justin Pollard
Nicoletta Pongan
Sarina Porgieter
Donna Potter
Dark Prince
Mark Pritchard
Anita Prosser
Danielle Proud
Ameen Rawat
Andrew Rawkins
Sarah Rayner
Sasha Reid
Monkey Joe Richards
Max Richardson
Miles Winter Roberts
Leanne Roberts-Hewitt
Sabine Roemer
Jade Kimberley Sylvia
    Rowlands
Laura Sainte Rose
Helene Sandberg
Jeremy Saunders
Dexter Say
Duncan Seddon
Terry Shand
So Shaw
Helen Sherborne
Alice Sinclair
Jeremy Singer

Mark Sloper
Jane Smith
Ross Smith
Cory Soutar
Paul Stacey
Sarah Steel
Julian Stewart Lindsay
Ralph St-Rose
Chris Sullivan
Steve Tabakin
Kasia Tauzowska
Diana Thompson
Ariel Vadee
Carla van den Berg
V vd lande
Tara Viesnik
Luis Villamizar
John Waddell
Katharine Walsh

Cara Ward
Alex Watson
Timo Weber
A.G. Wee
Katherine Wee
Lisa Wells
Oliver Wheeler
Jori White
Stevie Wilde
Harriet Williams
Rhodri Williams
Garry Wilson
Chris Woods
Steve Woodward
Hannah Wright
Marcia Wynter-Maharajh
James York
Elizabeth Yorke

A note about the typefaces

The main body text is set in the serif Garamond typeface. Named after punch-cutter Claude Garamond (1480–1561), who came from a family of French printers, it is widely acknowledged for its grace and fluidity, though Garamond himself is said to have claimed 'the art I practice is but a small thing'. Among its most definitive features are the small bowl of the a and narrow eye of the e, along with the crossed w. It is one of the most popular 'early' typefaces in the readily available catalogue of fonts in standard word-processing programmes, and is also one of the most eco-friendly typefaces for printing in terms of ink consumption.

Garamond's career began in 1540 with the commission to punch-cut the *grecs du roi*, a series of Greek letters which were used by Robert Estienne on behalf of the French king Francis I. In a more recent century, the iconic children's picture books of Dr. Seuss were set in a version of Garamond.

Garamond died in 1561 shortly after drawing up his will in which, after providing for his second wife, he instructed 'the surplus of all his goods' to be sold by a friend in order to pay for his elderly mother's care.

The running heads are set in Impact, designed in 1965 by Geoffrey Lee and produced by Stephenson Blake, the oldest and longest surviving type foundry in Britain which was active from 1818 until it finally closed in 2004. Impact is one of the world's most popular headline fonts, being highly visible and attention-grabbing.